BEYOND ORGASM

Dare to Be Honest

BEYOND

About the Sex

ORGASM

You Really Want

∽

Marty Klein, Ph.D.

Celestial Arts

Berkeley • Toronto

The records required by Section 2257 of Title 18 USC are kept by Celestial Arts, a
division of Ten Speed Press, 999 Harrison Street, Berkeley, California 94710.

CA

CELESTIAL ARTS
P.O. Box 7123
Berkeley, CA 94707
www.tenspeed.com

Distributed in Australia by Simon and Schuster Australia, in Canada by
Ten Speed Press Canada, in New Zealand by Southern Publishers Group,
in South Africa by Real Books, in Southeast Asia by Berkeley Books, and in
the United Kingdom and Europe by Airlift Book Company.

Cover design by Brad Greene
Text design by Felipe Lujan-Bear

Library of Congress Cataloging-in-Publication Data on file with the Publisher

First printing, 2002
Manufactured in the United States of America
1 2 3 4 5 6 7 8 9 10 – 09 08 07 06 05 04 03 02

Contents

෨෩

Other books by Dr. Marty Klein

Ask Me Anything: A Sex Therapist Answers the Most Important Questions

Let Me Count the Ways: Discovering Great Sex Without Intercourse

Sexual Intelligence: Politics, Culture, the Media, and Sex

Dr. Klein welcomes your comments on this book. You may contact him at Klein@SexEd.org. For articles, questions & answers, and more about Dr. Klein and his work, see his website at www.SexEd.org.

This book wouldn't have been written or published without Hal Bennett and Veronica Randall. More than simply agent and editor, they both understood and believed in my vision from the start. They are generous souls and rare professionals. They are actual book people.

෨෧

To those who have taught me to tell the truth—and who have the courage to live it themselves.

Introduction

❦❦

Y ou probably want to enjoy sex more. That's why you bought this
book, right? Lots of books tell you how to make sex better. (And most fail—
have you noticed?) That's not the approach in this one. Instead, you're
going to read about how to get more from sex—by bringing more to sex.

What would you need to enjoy sex more? Well, what makes enjoyable sex so enjoyable? For most of us, it's a combination of pleasure and
intimacy. But beyond that is the luxurious feeling of freedom, the letting go of limitations, the almost spiritual sense of wholeness that we
can create when we connect with our sexual selves and allow our lovers
to do the same. This is what gives sex value beyond the physical experience. The unique thing sex offers goes beyond pleasure and intimacy:
It's the option of being truly known, because for a few moments (maybe
even a few hours) you're actually willing to be yourself. What you'll discover in this book is that by being true to your sexuality, in fact, you can
be yourself every time you have sex. To the extent that we do so, we can
connect to another person (as well as to ourselves) in a special way, and
go beyond orgasm toward a new kind of sexual satisfaction.

All this requires relaxation, trust, and confidence—not that any given
sexual experience will be perfect, but rather that whatever happens during sex is going to be okay. To maintain a relaxed, trusting, confident

approach, a certain kind of partnership is almost essential, whether that partnership involves a long-term relationship or a temporary, even casual one. Yes, it's possible to create this partnership with someone you don't know very well, as long as both of you are committed to being yourselves, and have the skills to do so.

Whether you are in a thirty-year marriage or are considering a one-night stand, being yourself requires revealing your inner world—your preferences, thoughts, fantasies, experiences. This is easier, of course, when you approve of and are comfortable with these parts of yourself. But you can't always count on your own approval; in fact, we all, at times, disapprove of parts of who we are. This is one reason why it's so important to accept yourself, especially sexually. In the chapters that follow, you'll learn how to do so, a gift you'll be able to carry with you, and enjoy with your partners, for the rest of your life. Great sex starts when you look at your lover and say, "Here I am, come with me. I don't know where we're going, but we can't do anything wrong. After all, it's sex."

Revealing yourself to your partners on a continuing basis is not just about giving information to them. The experience of revealing yourself—the anxiety, the self-examination, the risk-taking, the pride—is part of enhancing your inner dialogue, the ongoing conversation you have with yourself. To take your sexuality beyond orgasm, you need to be sensitive to who you are—to who you're bringing to your bed and to your partner, to what you want, and to how you feel about all this. It begins when you stop worrying about being a great lover, and start wanting to be good partner.

So, if it's self-acceptance that makes self-revelation possible, why is it so difficult for so many of us? Self-rejection and sex-negativity nag at many of us to one degree or another from time to time. Generally learned in childhood, sexual self-rejection encourages isolation, depression, and keeping sexual secrets, resulting in the Secrecy Imperative, which we will explore in Chapter 3.

Sexual secret-keeping has one critical consequence that stands out above the rest: It limits how satisfying sex can be. Yes, you may still get hard or get wet when appropriate, and perhaps even come. But sexual secret-keeping prevents you from going beyond orgasm. That's why better sex—much, much better sex—starts with examining your sexual honesty.

In the next chapter we'll talk about orgasms—what they are, how we have them, why we like them, if they're the same for men and women, why we measure the quality of our sexual relationships and our skill as lovers by how big or frequent they are, and what lies beyond them.

Chapter 1

Orgasm—Friend or Foe?

෧෨

Orgasm: the perfect compromise between love and death.

—ROBERT BAK

What exactly is this experience that so many people like so much? For starters, there's the physical experience. Orgasm is a complex phenomenon with several aspects including:

◇ increased heart rate and breathing
◇ reddening of the skin, especially on the face and chest
◇ pelvic throbbing
◇ erection of the nipples and genitals
◇ heightened threshold of pain
◇ contractions of the muscles around the anus, vagina, prostate and elsewhere

Notice, by the way, that "exploding skyrockets" and "the earth moving out of its planetary orbit" are not included here.

Our brain translates these physical sensations into "pleasure." We enjoy the muscle tension and the release that follows. We enjoy the warmth that floods us, and even the fatigue that immediately follows.

1

We like the way our attention narrows, making us oblivious to everything outside our immediate experience. This has a physical basis, too, in the body's release of neurochemicals—hormones and other substances—into the bloodstream and brain.

Everyone has orgasms early in life—during infancy, childhood, and even before that, in the uterus. The sexual response system is triggered by hormones. Infants and young children orgasm from involuntary dreams and voluntary self-pleasuring. All of our organs prepare, in childhood, for adult function, and our sexual response is one of those organ systems.

In a sense, everyone's body has the same orgasm, with physical responses caused by identical processes. For example, our pelvic and anal muscles spasm at the identical rate—once every 8/10 of a second. Most men (along with a very small number of women) ejaculate, spurting fluid for a few moments. That said, each of us experiences orgasm slightly differently; you may or may not be one of those people whose face flushes, whose fingers and toes clutch, whose eyes roll, whose throat produces unexpected sounds.

At the same time, orgasm is an **emotional** experience, a burst of subjective feelings that many people value even more than its physical sensations. This is particularly true if we come without great effort or emotional conflict.

For example, orgasm is often accompanied by a moment of complete acceptance, if not downright love, of our body. No one has a bad hair day or feels overweight (or wrinkled, skinny, or dowdy) while they're coming. Even if you have a physique that isn't conventionally beautiful, during orgasm you *know* just how perfect your body is. For some of us, this is the most wonderful gift on earth.

Many people also feel a profound sense of wholeness or connectedness when they come: to nature, for example, to the universe, or to God. Another way to describe this state is wholeness. We feel ourselves to be whole, and yet we also feel a part of something larger than ourselves. Orgasm is paradoxical that way.

If we come with a partner, we may feel particularly close to him or her both during and after it. We may experience a variety of feelings all at once, including gratitude, generosity, compassion, vulnerability, understanding, trust, forgiveness, surrender, and love. Partners sometimes feel certain that both of them are feeling similar things at the same time. These are some of the reasons that many people like to cuddle and remain close after they come. It isn't just the unwinding of the physical experience; it's the "afterglow" involving our emotions.

Another way to describe this experience is weightlessness, both physical and psychological. During orgasm we let go of much of what prevents connection with another person, with ourselves—because the physical sensation is so intense it crowds out anxiety, self-criticism, and body self-consciousness. When we let go of what holds us down, we can more easily connect to our erotic selves: playful, passionate, accepting, and imaginative.

Wouldn't it be nice if we could have these feelings for more than two seconds at a time? Or if we could summon these feelings without going through the physical process of orgasm itself? There's an enormous range of erotic experiences available to us if we're willing to tune into our body, let go of our inhibitions, trust our partner, and expand our definitions of sexuality. This may very well require talking with our partners in new ways—before, during, even after being sexual together.

That's what this book is about. This book is going to help you create sex that's orgasmic even when you're not coming. So let's finish exploring orgasm. Then we'll talk about what lies beyond it, and how to get there.

Sexual mythology

Not surprisingly, there's a lot of misunderstanding and misinformation about orgasm. Let's look at the most common myths about it. Remember, a myth is an idea that everyone accepts, but **isn't true.**

MYTH #1: ORGASM IS THE GOAL OF SEX

Many of us aim for orgasm during sex. We single-mindedly pursue it, ignoring the subtleties and various directions lovemaking can go. When that's the case, not coming can be disappointing and even frustrating.

If this is your approach to sex, you're missing most of what sex has to offer. When you make orgasm the goal of sex, you're saying that a two-second experience is the main reason for ten minutes—or an hour, or however long you spend—of effort. What a waste of all that energy! No matter how dramatic, no orgasm can be big enough to compensate for the lack of good sex along the way. So enjoy your orgasm if and when you have it. But don't focus on it so much that you miss the context. Or else you might feel alone the second you're done, and that would be too bad.

If you're with a partner who thinks orgasm is the goal of sex, explain your perspective and invite him or her to join you in exploring alternatives.

MYTH #2: ORGASM IS BEST FROM INTERCOURSE

Why should our orgasms be strongest from intercourse? If you're a woman, you probably need clitoral stimulation to come, which intercourse can't offer (unless you or your partner uses a hand). If you're a man, intercourse may not provide the stimulation you prefer—your partner's vagina may be too wet, or too tight, or curved at an angle that just doesn't suit you. And the performance anxieties with which people torment themselves during intercourse can make the resulting orgasms less a thrill than a relief or disappointment.

Does it matter how you have an orgasm? For years, people have debated the "clitoral" vs. "vaginal" source of female orgasm. Some feel one is somehow more mature or womanly than the other. Well, which is more "womanly," vanilla ice cream or chocolate? Being left-handed or right-handed? It's all a matter of taste and of your body's programming.

Let's put an end to this sort of question, and restore the orgasmic focus where it belongs—on how it *feels*.

We even have some data about orgasmic preferences. In the 1970s, Shere Hite interviewed thousands of men and women about a range of sexual topics. One thing she found was that most people had their strongest orgasms from masturbation. The second strongest were typically during oral sex. Your experience may be different; perhaps it matches Hite's rather large sample.

MYTH #3: YOU SHOULD INHIBIT YOURSELF DURING ORGASM

Let's be honest about this: Most of us seem a little strange during orgasm. We groan, pant, drool, fart, swear, grab, demand, even cry. Do you look or sound silly when you come? Make promises you later want to renounce? Seem not quite yourself?

That's the whole point—to lose your mind—to leave your mind, and inhabit your body while it leaves the earth for a moment. Attempting to control this process can prevent it entirely. Attempting to retain consciousness while you come is like trying to sneeze with your eyes open. It can be done, but it doesn't feel complete, and it makes you wonder what it would be like if you didn't interfere with your body's natural rhythm.

MYTH #4: YOU OWE IT TO YOUR PARTNER TO CLIMAX DURING SEX
As if the question makes perfect sense, people frequently ask me, "How else is your partner supposed to know that you're having a good time? Or that he or she is a 'good lover'?"

Perhaps the best answer is that orgasm is too important to be used to validate someone else.

How should someone know you're enjoying the sex? He or she could ask you. Or look at your face, or notice how your body is reacting. Or kiss you and see how responsive you are. But some people are shy about asking, hesitant about kissing, and, well, too nervous to actually *notice* how you're doing. That's why they need a yardstick, something tangible to prove their adequacy or your pleasure.

What a shame. Feeling pressured to have an orgasm for someone else is a sure way to introduce self-consciousness, doubt, and resentment into a sexual situation—not to mention that it simply makes it harder to come. Try something altogether different—relax, be yourself, and just get really, really close to your lover's body and heart while you're sexual together.

If your partner "needs" your orgasm for him- or herself, you have a bigger problem than just orgasms, which you should discuss when you're **not** in bed. If you need your partner's orgasm in order to feel adequate, consider other ways you might get your emotional needs satisfied. Therapy might be of great benefit to you now and in future relationships.

A broader erotic vision

So what's beyond orgasm? What kind of sex are we going to talk about for the rest of this book?

For starters, we'll be talking about sexuality rather than sex. That simple distinction is a way of continually reminding ourselves that we're not just talking about intercourse, or genital sex, or orgasm, or "doing it." To really broaden our thinking and expand our minds, we need to think about eroticism in new ways.

This broader erotic vision that lies beyond orgasm may surprise you. It involves imagination, risk-taking, and a kind of intimacy that may be unfamiliar to you. This intimacy, by the way, is available in casual as well as committed relationships.

Ultimately, **being yourself** is absolutely critical to great sex. Ironically, this is both harder and easier to do than many people imagine. It requires no special equipment, no physical beauty or agility, no secret sexual knowledge or technique. It does, however, require that you be honest with yourself about who you really are: your interests, fantasies, past, and intentions. Once you can do that, asking for what you want and accepting it—if you get it—takes you close to the heart of great sex. When you can experiment sexually—either alone or with a partner— without fearing the loss of your relationship, self-esteem, or sense of masculinity or femininity, you're just about there. And when you can turn everything into a sex game, when everything is erotic (even emotional vulnerability), then you can't **help** but have great sex.

So how do you create this kind of sex? Turn the page. We'll talk about secrecy, trust, and communication. How are they connected? How do they determine the kind of sex we have?

Chapter 2

Why Do We Hide Our Sexuality? Why Do You?

๑๑

It may be called the master passion, the hunger for self-approval.

—MARK TWAIN

Sexually, are you normal? If I had to guess, I'd say yes. And that's without knowing what you do, how often you do it, with whom you do it, or how well you do it.

Surprised? Almost everyone seems to wonder if they're sexually normal. When it comes to other activities, of course, we know how we measure up. For example, we watch other people eat, drive, buy clothes, prepare meals, and discipline their children. We can compare ourselves to family, friends, and strangers doing these things, and usually we decide that we're okay.

But sex? Which real people can we watch? Who can we talk with honestly? As a result, we often compare ourselves to the media images that surround us of unrealistic beauty, boundless self-confidence, perfect functioning, dependable desire—and plenty of time to enjoy it all. Is it any wonder that we seem to fall short by comparison?

For years now, people have asked me for measurements of sexual normalcy—which I've generally refused to give. Instead of using statistics, I'd rather you decide that you're sexually normal based on a warm sense of self-acceptance. One of my principal reasons for writing this book is to give you information, guidelines, and encouragement for accepting yourself.

Let's start with a simple checklist that illustrates the wide range of sexually normal behavior. You are **not abnormal,** just because you:

◇ have sex once a day, or once every four months
◇ have only one sex partner in a lifetime, or a dozen different partners each year
◇ masturbate every day, or not at all—regardless of your relationship status
◇ think about someone other than your partner during sex—even someone completely off-limits
◇ never fantasize about sex
◇ acquire a sexually transmitted disease
◇ prefer oral or manual sex to intercourse, or vice versa
◇ enjoy many different positions, or the same routine every time
◇ are ashamed of your body, or proud of it
◇ enjoy pornography, erotica, or romance novels, or are turned off by them
◇ feel excited or depressed about the sexual changes aging brings, or not notice any changes
◇ notice your sexual preferences and feelings change during the course of a month, or a year
◇ have erection or orgasm problems
◇ find it difficult to discuss your feelings or preferences, even with the person to whom you are closest
◇ have been victimized through rape, forced sex, or childhood exploitation
◇ wonder if you're normal

It doesn't matter where on this list you locate yourself. We all have our favorite colors, ice cream flavors, and TV shows, preferences we accept without question. It would be nice to accept our own sexual preferences and interests—and our lovers'—as easily.

Why does normalcy rate its own discussion? Because concerns about normalcy lie behind much of the self-rejection and secrecy discussed in the following chapters. I believe there would be far less anguish in our world if more people knew that they are sexually normal.

Concerns about sexual normality are the inevitable result of the way American children learn about sex. Most of us are **trained** to feel abnormal about our sexuality. We are **taught** to feel that our curiosity and our questions are bad. Naturally, we feel obliged to hide our sexual thoughts, feelings, and behavior.

The chapters that follow will challenge the way you've learned to think about sex, perhaps even the very meaning of sexuality itself. My goal is to help you **own** your sexuality as a wholesome entity. Once you accomplish that, you can then decide how to handle specific issues. You can pursue your curiosity about S/M or keep it in the realm of fantasy. You can tell your partner you like your anus stimulated or just hope you happen to get touched there. You can decide what to keep private and what to share.

We'll examine such questions as: What is healthy sexuality? What is a healthy relationship? We'll also begin to look at **patterns** in our relationships, patterns that are often invisible to those most affected by them. This book will help make them visible so we can understand and decide what to do about them.

We frequently complain or get depressed about our relationship frustrations. Rarely do we take control of our destiny and examine, discuss, and create change in the relationship routines that cause our frustration.

Why do we fear relationships?

We all, on some level, have fear about relationships. We learn about relationships as infants, when our needs are simple: to be kept warm, dry, and fed. When these needs are gratified, we experience relating to others as good. At other times, when our needs are frustrated, we learn that relating—that is, depending on others—is a mistake.

As long as our basic needs are reasonably satisfied, we can handle the frustrations. As psychologist D. W. Winnicott explained, parents do not have to be perfect caregivers; they merely have to be "good enough." Interacting with "good enough" parents helps give us a positive attitude about closeness. We trust that our relationships will generally be satisfying, and that the inevitable bumps will be relatively short-lived.

Unfortunately, the relative inexperience of most parents, coupled with the characteristic innocence of the human infant's mind, seems to conspire against developing this general sense of safety. The still-incomplete brain cannot adequately cope with the everyday irritability, insecurity, or disappointments expressed by parents in the normal routine of living. Babies are not sophisticated enough to imagine that their own frustration may be the result of a parent's nonresponsiveness, rather than their own inadequacies.

Here lies the terrible conflict of infancy: to be self-centered and demanding at the same time that we are 100 percent dependent on the good will of others. The dependency is literal, for if the caregivers withdraw too much of their attention the infant will, in fact, die.

In this sense, babies experience situations in only one of two ways: A given moment either contributes to gratification, or it threatens total destruction. This need for immediate satisfaction is as complex as the undeveloped infant mind gets. If you've ever tried to encourage a baby to stop crying while you fix a bottle, you've experienced this firsthand.

Infants experience the threat of their own destruction in three forms: 1) "I'll be annihilated," 2) "I'll be suffocated," and 3) "I'll be abandoned." We carry this heritage with us all our lives. More than simply damaging our later relationships, it characterizes and partially determines them.

Thus, we enter adult relationships unconsciously afraid of being destroyed. Not just afraid of being rejected or hurt, but afraid of being **destroyed.**

Sexual secrecy

We live in a world that encourages sexual secrets. These secrets don't protect us or make our lives better the way they are supposed to. On the contrary, these secrets only cripple our true sexual self, which is hidden, ignored, denied, and distorted.

As a result, girls punish themselves for erotic thoughts about father or big brother. Boys furtively hide evidence of wet dreams. Both sexes try desperately not to masturbate. Everyone feels guilty.

Is there an eight-year-old somewhere who has no sexual secrets from Mom or Dad? Is there a thirty-eight-year old anywhere who keeps no sexual secrets from spouse, lover, or best friend?

Now we understand that the two questions are virtually one, for the foundations of adult behavior are laid in childhood. Sexual learning, in particular, begins at birth.

How do we come to develop secrets about sex? When does this happen, and why? What exactly are sexual secrets anyway?

Sexual secrecy is much broader than simple lying. Most of the clients with whom I work have found this a useful definition: **Sexual secret-keeping takes place whenever you withhold information about your** *sexuality from relevant others. It also takes place when you allow a significant person in your life to believe misinformation or make incorrect assumptions about your sexuality, regardless of where the mistaken ideas come from.*

"Self-secrecy" occurs when our true feelings are so unacceptable to us that we unconsciously cover them with other feelings. Many men, for example, cannot admit to themselves that they fear women's powerful sexuality. One way to express this fear is through constant criticism—of housekeeping skills, spending habits, sense of humor, and career commitment of a wife or girlfriend. Ironically, the isolation of secret-keeping magnifies the fear and intensifies the inner conflict.

Every relationship has unspoken expectations about communication, trust, and closeness that help define secrecy for the people involved. Say that you've had a vasectomy. Not mentioning this during a one-night stand is one thing. Not disclosing it to a fiancée is quite another. Allowing her to assume, by your silence, that you are fertile can create enormous problems—guilt and anxiety in the present, disappointment, conflict and possibly divorce in the future.

Trust in relationships is vulnerable to both honest disagreement and not-so-honest manipulation. Everyone has a sexual history, sexual feelings, and sex-related beliefs. Do you and your partner agree on which of these are relevant to your relationship?

If your definition of "relevant information" has ever differed from someone else's, you've probably been told (or said) things like "How could you not tell me?" or "What do you mean you figured what I didn't know couldn't hurt me?" or "No, I don't understand that it just never came up." Such comments reflect anger and humiliation. That's how we feel when we no longer know where we stand, or what our relationships' agreements are. When our sense of reality is challenged, we lose our sense of what things mean. And we fear the confusion that awaits us in the days that follow. Most couples and individuals have unstated expectations about communication regarding the following. What are yours?

⋄ Which subjects are you not supposed to raise with each other?
⋄ Which aspects of the relationship are you not to discuss with anyone else?
⋄ How should disagreements be handled?
⋄ How should affection be expressed?
⋄ How do you get each other's attention?
⋄ How is criticism best delivered?
⋄ How do you each handle feeling misunderstood?

In our culture, every conceivable aspect of sexuality is subject to secrecy. Common sexual secrets include faked orgasms, extramarital relationships, fantasies about making love with a person of the same sex, and the experience of having been exploited in childhood.

Recently, I asked some of my students to think of a sex-related subject that no one hides. Take a moment right now and try this yourself.

Brainstorming in small groups, they found themselves stymied. Finally, a likely candidate emerged: the enjoyment of sex itself. But even this simple acknowledgment is subject to secrecy.

Many of us are taught, for example, that women don't really enjoy sex. They either like the closeness, one tradition goes, or they use sex to acquire and manipulate husbands. I have counseled many women who feared they were "oversexed" because they had a strong, healthy sex drive, or because they openly enjoy sexual pleasure. As a result of traditional pressures, many women hide their interest in sex from friends, men in general, the man or woman they're involved with, and even themselves. So we can't really say that "I like sex" is never a sexual secret.

Some students suggested that the simple admission of having sex is never subject to secrecy. But we realized that many people hide that too, including teens, unmarried and widowed adults, nuns, and senior citizens. Most nursing homes, in fact, report that the adult children of their residents expect the staff to discourage sexual activity.

Several other possibilities were considered but rejected. They included "I'm a virgin," "I hate homosexuals," "I like my body," "I want to get pregnant," and "You turn me on." The class had to admit they couldn't think of a single aspect of sexuality that somebody somewhere isn't hiding from themselves or others.

Certain themes did, however, emerge. Thus, the categories of sexual secrets we will look at in Chapters 4 through 7 are:

⋄ Arousal and response
⋄ Fantasies and feelings
⋄ The past
⋄ Deliberate deception

Why secrecy?

We know that we keep sexual secrets primarily because we fear that we aren't sexually normal, which leads us to reject our own eroticism. There are many folk explanations for sexual secret-keeping. On close examination, the obvious ones are inadequate, so let's look at these first.

EXPLANATION 1: SECRECY IS "NATURAL"

American society distorts and discourges so many of what should be our "natural" expressions of sexuality: for example, we learn that gentleness in men, assertiveness in women, sensuous nongenital touching, guilt-free enjoyment of masturbation, and the ability to celebrate monogamy are considered "unnatural."

And yet, other cultures around the world and throughout history consider these expressions to be perfectly natural. So even if sexual secrecy were, in fact, "natural," that wouldn't make it any more likely to appear in our behavior.

Nor are all American forms of sexual expression thought to be "natural" by the rest of the world's standards. Many tribal cultures are far more permissive than ours—the Dani in Papua New Guinea are reported to have practically no sexual taboos, except for the rule preventing members of the two main clans from having sex with each other. In many Scandinavian families, children and parents routinely acknowledge and discuss sexual behavior. They consider our embarrassment, secrecy, and denial quite backward—and, by the way, they have a teen pregnancy rate a small fraction of ours.

These societies contrast starkly with Inis Beag, an Irish island described by anthropologist John C. Messenger as the most erotically barren place on earth. Marriages there are arranged, and premarital sex is unknown. Adults do not bathe themselves between neck and knee. Considered indulgent, breast-feeding is rare. And sex is only for procreation: Men feel debilitated by the loss of their semen, while women endure sex as a distasteful duty.

These particular cultures have differing ideas about the "naturalness" of secrecy. In fact, the dramatically different norms of these societies argue eloquently against using "naturalness" to explain *any* sexual behavior. "Natural" sexuality? No one in our modern age can ever, unfortunately, know what that is.

As Leonore Tiefer writes in *Sex Is Not A Natural Act*, "Human sexuality is not a biological given and cannot be explained in terms of reproductive biology or instinct . . . What is done, when, where, by whom, with whom, with what, and why—these things have almost nothing to do with [natural] biology."

EXPLANATION 2: HUMAN SEXUALITY IS UGLY, BAD
OR DESTRUCTIVE, AND SHOULD BE HIDDEN

Our nineteenth-century ancestors were so obsessed with the destructive power of sex that they saw its dangers everywhere. They covered the legs of furniture, for example, for fear that men would be reminded of women's legs and get aroused. And they renamed the breasts and thighs of poultry so families wouldn't need to speak such words. Did you know that that's why we now refer to white meat and dark meat?

Laughable though these customs may seem, many people who oppose modern sex education share the same underlying attitude. They believe that if we don't tightly control the sexuality of adolescents, it will run wild and destroy us all. These fearful people have even arranged for their local high school libraries to ban such books as *The Diary of Anne Frank*, *The Color Purple*, and *Catcher in the Rye*. Despite the examples of Hitler's Germany and Stalin's Soviet Union, they are convinced that secrecy can protect them.

The Bible is frequently invoked to justify sexual secrecy, but when it is, one wonders which Bible is being used. Could it be the Bible that celebrates God's creation of our bodies? The Bible of Solomon's erotic *Song of Songs*? The Bible that talks of passionate love between husband and wife, and between David and Jonathan? Some people use the Bible the way others use astrology—to justify whatever beliefs and feelings they bring to it.

Fear of sexuality leads to the belief that sex is bad and secrecy is good. These beliefs, however, are destructive and spiritually empty. Facing and letting go of sexual fear is a healthier, more life-affirming choice.

EXPLANATION 3: OUR PARTNERS CAN'T HANDLE OUR SECRETS

Many of us believe, correctly or not, that our partners are unable to handle sexual honesty. This makes sharing secrets seem like a poor idea, while secrecy looks like a good way of protecting our lover and ourselves. This explanation is usually accompanied by "good" reasons such as:

- ◇ "Anyone with my background is a slut, and no man wants a slut."
- ◇ "Her ego is too fragile."
- ◇ "It would remind him of his awful first marriage."
- ◇ "It would destroy her to know the truth."
- ◇ "He'd kill my father."

But there's something suspicious here. My research reveals that most of us believe that **we** could handle the truth about our **partner's** sexuality. Yet we believe that our **partner** can't handle similar truths about **us.**

We aren't **all** stuck with a lover who is less open than we are. In many cases, our beliefs about someone else's inflexibility are more about us than they are about the other person. These judgments tend to be tenacious, persisting in the face of what would be contrary evidence if only we were willing to see it.

Do you believe your husband or boyfriend just can't handle the truth about you? Have you checked it out with him? Would you know if you were wrong? Could you allow your wife or girlfriend to be more tolerant than you imagined? How would your life change if you found out she **could** handle your secret?

Can you take **yes** for an answer?

An alternative explanation

Assume for a moment that we keep secrets to **protect ourselves.** From what? From the negative consequences of sexuality that we're trained, as children, to expect.

Most American children are taught that their innocent sexuality is "bad." You may have learned this lesson by growing up in a home where sex was never discussed, or spoken about only scornfully. You may recall specific moments when you learned that sexuality is dangerous: when you asked a sexual question and were humiliated, for example, or when you were punished for masturbating.

Here are some of the ways we absorb negativity about sex while we are growing up:

⬦ We are caught and punished simply for expressing our sexuality. Perhaps you were caught masturbating, or found playing "doctor" and touching a friend's genitals as a child.

⬦ We are told directly by parents, teachers, and other adults that sex is bad. When my neighbor June was a child, for example, she was frequently warned by an aunt that "Boys only want one thing—to touch you under your clothes." Although June didn't understand quite why, she says, "My aunt's tone made it clear that this was a horrible thing." A related message you may have been told is that any girl who enjoys "that sort of thing" is a "tramp." "I didn't know what that meant either," says June, "but it was obviously bad."

⬦ We observe our parents' behavior toward each other. If there is no physical affection, if one parent typically pushes the other's hand away, if one parent criticizes the other's sexual references or gestures, an observing child learns that sex is not a nice thing for people to share.

⬦ We experience our parents' discomfort in relating to our genitals. They give them funny names (like "woo-woo," or worse, "down there"), refuse to touch or wash them, and discourage questions about them. This contrasts sharply with the matter-of-fact approach often taken with the rest of our body.

⋄ We notice the way sex education is handled. Many schools offer no "education" on the subject whatsoever. They present dangerous "abstinence training" programs using blatant lies, scare tactics, and religious ideas packaged as curriculum, which urges kids to refrain from sex altogether. Studies by both professional sexologists and the federal government agree that these programs do nothing to reduce sexual behavior or teen pregnancy, while undermining children's understanding of and comfort with their bodies and sexual feelings.

Too many local activists and school officials are joined in a baffling alliance to deny children the information they need to make healthy sexual choices and lead healthy lives. Kids are smart enough to know this, but they aren't sophisticated enough to understand why. They come to the obvious conclusion that sex is bad, or that something about it is wrong and must be hidden. Some even decide that if sex is so evil it must be the perfect way to express anger against adults—to everyone's detriment.

⋄ We participate in religions that are interpreted in antisexual ways. Masturbation and sexual fantasy are still considered sinful by many faiths and denominations—perhaps yours. This means that virtually 100 percent of the children from these religious backgrounds are labeled sinners, and feel guilty.

⋄ We are bombarded with mass entertainment and advertising that is basically antisexual. The media exploit and distort sexual curiosity and interest; check any soap opera or beer ad. But at the same time, they fail to present sexuality as it really is. They could do this, for example, through contraceptive ads or the appropriate, casual mention of birth control in programming.

When sexuality is seriously discussed in the media, it is generally presented as part of a problem, such as AIDS or teen pregnancy. Eroticism is rarely portrayed as something to celebrate, such as the way it enhances relationships, or its spiritual dimension, or the way touching has humanized health care environments.

In all, the lessons Americans learn about sex during childhood are consistently negative and destructive.

The secrecy imperative

In these different ways, sex is linked with shame, guilt, fear, and anxiety. Learning that sex in general is destructive, children apply that judgment to their own sexuality. Their simplistic moralism combines with their simplistic logic; they think, "Sex is bad. I am sexual. Therefore I am bad." Thus, sexuality is a focus of punishment and rejection, and the expression of personal inadequacy.

The experience of parental rejection over sexual issues has a profound impact. As we've already seen, children are keenly aware that their very survival depends on the care and good will of their parents. Thus, kids fear that disapproval will be followed by abandonment—and death. (This legacy is one reason that many American adults are so phobic about rejection.)

Along with the young of every other species, human children are programmed for one thing: survival. And if they believe survival requires hiding this problematic thing called sex, they will do so. This is the origin of what I call the Secrecy Imperative: **The belief that to survive, you must hide your sexual thoughts, feelings, and behavior.** It's a sensible coping skill for surviving in an inexplicably hostile environment. This belief may or may not be conscious. In adulthood, the survival it attempts to ensure is psychological, rather than physical—which is every bit as meaningful.

So years before puberty, young people develop sexual secrets. Freud believed that the time between roughly six and eleven years of age is a "latency period." To gain distance from their own incestuous and aggressive drives, children "sublimated" their sexual energy into schoolwork and chores. Research studies from around the world collected in Sandford and Rademakers' 2000 book, *Childhood Sexuality: Normal Sexual Behavior and Development*, challenge that notion. Ronald and Juliette Goldman's enormous cross-cultural study shows that children **continue** developing their sexual interests, concepts, and vocabulary during this time. They simply do it as far from adult discovery as possible, having learned the rules of the adult world. Thus they continue to maintain the sexual secrecy that is already a fact of life.

This leads to enormous internal conflict. We continue to learn the adult values that promise survival, which contradict the wisdom we sense from our bodies and hearts. For example, how many of the following stifling guidelines do you remember hearing?

- ◇ "It's not ladylike to sit with your legs open."
- ◇ "Real men don't cry."
- ◇ "Remember, boys only want one thing from girls."
- ◇ "If a girl lets you touch her, she's not 'nice.' "
- ◇ "When they say 'no' they really mean 'yes.' "
- ◇ "You'd better do it, or he'll leave you for another girl."

The child's unsophisticated mind sees the world in simple black-and-white contrasts. We tend to overlearn the lessons of childhood. So not surprisingly, secrecy continues to evolve in adolescence. Increasingly self-aware, teenagers develop an additional pattern: secrecy from self.

Many young women, for example, refuse to carry condoms or a diaphragm on a date, unable to admit to themselves that they are considering having intercourse. Later that night, feeling passion's urgency or a sense of obligation, they acquiesce to unprotected sex. As educator Carol Cassell notes in *Swept Away*, they rationalize this as something that has happened **to** them, rather than as a situation they have helped create.

Our personal inventory of secrets continues to grow during sexual maturity. The Secrecy Imperative operates even as we create intimate, long-term relationships with both lovers and friends. There is a simple logic to what we keep hidden away: "If it's about my sexuality, it's probably not okay."

It doesn't even matter how reasonable or enjoyable the behavior is. The capacity for multiple orgasms, for example, can be deeply satisfying. But it may also contradict a self-image of demure, controlled, ladylike behavior. Sadly, I have spoken to many women who felt it was necessary to hide this exciting part of their sexuality, or even abandon it altogether.

This is the result of a profound suspicion of being "bad." Since we cannot accept ourselves, we cannot imagine being accepted by someone else. That is why most of us say, "Yes, I could probably handle my lover's sexual secrets, but I don't think my lover could handle mine."

Most of us believe, unconsciously, that we **must** keep sexual secrets, still attempting to survive as we did when children. The Secrecy Imperative, then, is why sexual secrecy is so ubiquitous. Psychological survival depends on it in childhood, and we never lose the commitment to it as we mature. As adults living in a profoundly antisexual culture, why should we?

How does secrecy produce
the illusion of safety?

In spite of our fears, we still have the need to relate. The human animal needs others to speak with and bond with, to touch, be touched by, and to nurture and be nurtured by. Without these, we grow physically and emotionally ill.

The human dilemma, therefore, is this: How can I fulfill my need to relate while also protecting myself from the perceived threat of annihilation? And how can I do this without somehow pushing away those who are close to me, and destroying the magical relationships I need to survive?

Many of us solve this existential problem unconsciously in the way we construct our intimate relationships. We choose a format that allows us to be **somewhat** close when we most want to, while allowing us to deny or destroy the closeness when that feels necessary.

You'd have to create such a relationship in a particular way. You'd have to avoid being real enough for someone else to truly know you, pin you down, and possibly destroy you. You'd have to develop and relate through a pseudo-self—a contrived image of a person rather than a whole, real person.

Sexual secrecy is a common way to accomplish this. It allows you to manipulate who your partner thinks you are. It's easy to justify doing this, because of the unspoken cultural agreement that we can't handle each other's sexual feelings, thoughts, and behavior.

Keep in mind that this strategy only makes you *feel* safer. You don't get the intimacy of real acceptance. You only get the pseudo-intimacy of feeling safe from attack.

There are four ways in which sexual secrecy lets us feel safer and less frightened of being destroyed while relating. These ways allow us to:

1. Seize power.
2. Create distance.
3. Act out feelings.
4. Fulfill the demands of unconscious childhood scripts.

Use these overlapping categories to examine how **you** value secrecy.

SEIZE POWER

As a secret-keeper, you can seize power by influencing various aspects of closeness, such as the level of trust, nurturance, sexual satisfaction, and cooperation.

Secrecy can also be a way of controlling information. You can decide what your partner will know about you and your relationship. Through secrecy you can give yourself a different past, and therefore control the direction of the present.

Another way in which secrecy can be used to seize power is in the creation and maintenance of a personal treasure—some fact, experience, feeling, or object that only you control. The treasure can be so personal that no one else knows it even exists. Examples could be a sexual encounter with someone famous, or your interest in cross-dressing when out of town on business.

Finally, secrecy can make relationships seem safer by the power it gives you to limit sexual bonding, which may feel dangerous or dirty.

The story of a software designer I once worked with illustrates this well. Although she had great difficulty reaching orgasm with her boyfriend Dan, Tammy refused to tell him what kind of touching aroused her most. "He should know by now," she insisted. "Besides, it's so unromantic. 'A little to the left. Now harder. Now slower.' The whole idea turns me off."

Tammy was very frustrated about what she called the "incompleteness" of the sex she had with Dan. Yet, she only did the homework I assigned about half the time. She sometimes came to our sessions late, and even left early for a dinner appointment once. When I questioned her about such behavior, she shrugged it off.

Obviously, some part of Tammy did not want the sexual problem fixed, but it wouldn't have been helpful for me to come right out and say that. So I asked her to close her eyes and imagine a scene from her future, after the successful completion of therapy.

"Imagine that it is six months from now, Tammy, and your orgasm problem is solved." I paused to let her get into the fantasy. "But you seem unhappy," I suggested. "Your shoulders are slumped, your face is frowning, and your legs are tightly crossed. Clearly, having orgasms easily has created other problems. What's wrong?"

"Dan knows all my tricks now," said Tammy, speaking from her imagined future. "He's used to me coming every time. And he wants sex a lot." I asked Tammy what that was like. "He's taking it for granted," she said. "Sex is taking over. He thinks whenever he wants to love me we can just go to bed and have a good time."

We were finally getting to the bottom of things. "And what's the matter with that?" I asked.

"It's not right," she replied, "the two of us just making love, as if there were nothing wrong with it. But there is. Sex can take over, turn you into a slave."

Tammy's unconscious had spoken: Her fantasy of life without sexual secrecy was full of pressure and danger. So Tammy had a good reason to prevent sex from becoming too enjoyable. She was using her avoidance and withholding to "survive" the dangers of sexuality.

Of course, the reality was that she was in no danger of becoming a "sex slave" to Dan. But Tammy's unconscious—like everyone else's—had a "reality" all its own. The task of therapy was to defuse the unnecessary fear it produced.

That's just what happened. Once Tammy was less afraid of bonding sexually with Dan, she was much more willing to share her secret—her "tricks" as she called them.

Secrecy sometimes does create the illusion of power in relationships. We'll discuss the incomplete and sometimes destructive nature of this power later on.

CREATE DISTANCE

Secrecy is also a way to create distance. For those who fear closeness, the ability to do this feels critically important. You might, unconsciously, want to create distance when your partner is offering support, such as empathy, affection, or practical help. For example, refusing to tell a current partner that you had been raped by a previous one—and that you had fears about being victimized again—would create distance and reduce an unconscious concern about being too dependent.

One way we create distance through sexual secrecy is by adopting the role of martyr. One man I worked with used to complain quite loudly about "having" to give his wife oral sex.

"Martha doesn't know how much I dislike the smell and taste of her pussy," Harold told me. "But since she enjoys me eating her so much, I do it. The whole thing feels yucky, though. God, being married is no picnic."

Harold never discussed his feelings with Martha, and his frustration grew. It was really a painful situation for him. At the same time, though, his martyr role fit like a comfortable shoe. It provided a "reason" for him not to be close, and for their sex together to be adversarial rather than shared.

Secret longing for a former lover or past relationship can also create distance. It can make a present partner or relationship look gray and uninviting, reducing your interest in sexual contact. This can chill a relationship, holding the other person at a more comfortable distance.

If you fear being suffocated or engulfed in relationships, you may develop the pattern of hiding from those close to you. The childhood belief here is: The only way I can have something all my own is by withholding it from the world. The "something" can be as simple as a favorite seashell or as complex as the right to choose a career.

Phil is a good example of this dynamic. Phil enjoyed watching sexually explicit videotapes, and had a large collection of them. But he kept this hobby a secret from everyone, and continued hiding it when his lover David moved in.

Although Phil admitted he had no reason to fear David's judgment, he was unwilling to take the risk of sharing his videos. "What will I do," asked Phil, "if he's turned off?" He refused to take such a chance, even though the two of them had enjoyed X-rated films at theaters together several times.

Phil's decision to keep a secret was an effective way of controlling the distance in the relationship. It resulted in his feeling alone, separate from David, guilty, and even resentful. It limited the quality of their sex together. And while none of this felt good, the situation did feel safer, in an odd way.

"Look, the bottom line is just me," he said once. "Why take chances on someone else's feelings? I know I can count on me, and I'd rather not worry about other people making my life complicated."

ACT OUT FEELINGS

One way our unconscious attempts to help us survive is by instructing us to hold back from expressing certain feelings directly. Expressing feelings *indirectly* through actions is called *acting out.*

The most common feeling that we act out through secrecy is anger. The infantile part of us fears we will be abandoned or destroyed if we express anger directly, so we express it covertly. We do this through the effects that secrets have, such as hurting someone or breaking an agreement. Such effects subtly gratify the anger that our unconscious believes is too dangerous to express directly. Other feelings that we sometimes act out through sexual secrecy include fear, grief, jealousy, despair, and competitiveness.

Let's look at the way acting out can be an unconscious solution to the conflict between needing and fearing closeness. The speaker is a struggling actress I'll call Lynette, who recently came to see me about her "endless frustrations." During our third session, she described an incident from the previous weekend.

"My husband Karl and I were out shopping together, and I ran into an old friend named Jay. We all got along nicely; in fact, we sat for almost an hour having coffee. Later, Karl asked how I knew Jay, and I made up a story about acting classes."

I nodded and said nothing. Lynette continued, "The truth is that Jay and I used to sleep together before I married Karl. I feel guilty about having lied, but I just wasn't prepared to tell the truth."

When I asked why, Lynette had several logical reasons. But there was very little feeling in her voice until she added, with a shrug, "Besides, Karl is no angel. Ask him about the teller who used to work at our bank's merchant window. Or the one who works there now, for that matter."

Suddenly Lynette's voice had life, so I pursued this. Apparently she felt that Karl had occasional affairs with other women. Had she tried to work out her resentment about this with Karl before? "Yes," she said with a trace of bitterness. She had confronted him with her suspicions, but never received much of an answer. "He's always saying how he wants me to be happy, but when I'd tell him what was bothering me, he'd become impatient with me. Finally I figured it was just a waste of time."

Noting this, I moved on to Lynette's other relationships. After asking a few questions, I saw that she had this same sense of powerlessness and unimportance with her father, her first husband, and her employer. And with her previous therapist. What was this pattern about?

"You get mad at people, they can't handle it," she said at one point. "No one wants to know what you **really** think, no matter what they say. I've made that mistake before, and I'll never do it again." Lynette was working hard to survive by burying her anger, but it had to go somewhere. How convenient to have sexual secrets, such as the one about Jay, with which to humiliate Karl and help her feel she had the upper hand.

The problem here isn't simply Lynette's lying, it's her belief that certain feelings endanger closeness. Once Lynette works that out—by resolving her leftover fears about being abandoned—she'll be able to make more rational decisions about how to relate to those she cares about.

Acting out is not usually a productive psychological compromise. Although you feel better for a moment, you virtually guarantee that the problem bothering you will return in the future.

FULFILL SCRIPT DEMANDS

The idea that each of us follows personal life scripts was developed by Dr. Eric Berne in the early 1960s. According to his theories of Transactional Analysis, these scripts come from decisions we make early in childhood. Designed to help us survive, these decisions lead to adult beliefs and character styles that restrict our ability to live flexible, free lives, responsive to the opportunities and demands of the moment.

No one consciously chooses to go along with a script. In fact, it is rare to have even an inkling of what your scripts are. Yet, aware or not, we make choices throughout our lives that fulfill the roles laid out in these scripts.

Everyone is familiar with the pop culture "archetypes" that have crept into the vernacular: the Peter Pan, who won't grow up; the Doormat, who lets people walk all over her and never protests; and the Angry Young Man, who would rather criticize than be nurtured. Let's look at some scripts that can be fulfilled by sexual secrecy:

- ◇ "I'm not really loveable, and never will be."
- ◇ "I'm a bad person."
- ◇ "I'm always being victimized or abused by those around me."
- ◇ "I must protect people who hurt me."
- ◇ "It's my job to keep peace and make sure no one's upset."
- ◇ "Women don't enjoy sex."
- ◇ "Men and women are never sexually compatible."
- ◇ "For gay people, sex will always be complicated."
- ◇ "I will die heroically."
- ◇ "I'm not important enough for anyone to care about."
- ◇ "Men/women will love me for my mind but be bored with my looks."

In Chapters 4 through 7, we will look at dozens of sexual secrets that help fulfill these various scripts. For now, let's look at an example of how scripts and secrets are connected.

Here is a very common script that people often play out in nonsexual ways. In the example that follows, it was played out sexually.

SCRIPT: "I've always got some kind of emotional problem—life would be empty without one."
SECRET: "I have herpes."

Maurice has had herpes for six years. Through a combination of medication and group therapy, he has brought it under control. Now

Maurice has only one or two outbreaks a year.

Nevertheless, he hides his condition from his sexual partners, claiming to be "just not in the mood" when he is contagious. Given the chance, any of his girlfriends over the years might have simply accepted the fact of his herpes. They could have gone for joint counseling, if necessary, or specifically focused on "safer sex."

But Maurice is stuck on his herpes. He **needs** to be, because a serious relationship without a disturbing problem is too scary for him. It makes him feel vulnerable, makes him feel the relationship is about to overwhelm and carry him away, and that he has no anchor.

By keeping the herpes a secret, Maurice makes it a problem. This allows him to participate in a relationship with less fear—to "survive." And it allows him to extend his belief in the myth surrounding his script, which is, "If I could only clear up my problem, life could be great."

It's hard for us to see our own scripts because we're living inside them. Still, you can ask yourself: What are the ongoing themes in my life? What seems inevitable to me? What are my family's myths about me? What was I born for?

Chapter 3

The High Cost of Secrecy

◎◎

He felt separate, alone, not able to reach out to anyone. So he bought a book called How to Hug—*and discovered, when he got home, that it was volume 9 of the encyclopedia.*

—MORT SAHL

S exual secrecy in relationships is a trade-off. By helping you feel less vulnerable to judgment and rejection, it can reduce the emotional turmoil you feel about intimacy, allowing you to enter and maintain relationships. But as we've seen, secrecy also limits the depth and satisfaction of relationships. This is the price for that always-temporary peace of mind. This chapter examines four problems associated with sexual secret-keeping:

⬧ How do secrets isolate us from those we love?
⬧ How do secrets lower our self-esteem?
⬧ How do secrets contribute to sexual problems?
⬧ How do secrets prevent the healing of emotional wounds?

We will explore each of these through the words and experiences of people who have struggled with them.

Isolation

As we have seen, keeping sexual information from your mate in today's environment is an understandable, very human thing to do. It's sometimes so automatic that you're not even aware you're doing it. This does not mean, however, that it's a harmless activity.

Withholding leads to isolation from our mates because it prevents us from being known for who we really are. And the more we hold back, the more we become isolated from ourselves, as our fear of discovery inhibits self-expression, especially during sex.

Secrecy also leads to isolation because it prevents the healing of traumatic sexual experiences from the past. This is significant because about one in five American families is touched by some form of sexual exploitation or violence. Too many of these crimes remain hidden, because many victims never tell a single soul.

Ultimately, secrecy makes sex a dangerous activity, because this is the likeliest place your secret will be discovered. Ordinarily, the pleasure and closeness of sex invite you to relax and let go each time you make love. But if you're busy concealing things, you **must** fear the way that every form of sexual expression—such as unusual turn-ons or low desire —might give you away.

When you keep secrets, even your sexual partners become adversaries. Those closest to you become the most threatening, always on the verge of stumbling onto your secret. Emotional withdrawal is the only "sensible" solution. Feelings of isolation and alienation are inevitable.

This is exactly what happened to one of my clients caught in the isolation trap. Gail fidgeted throughout her first session; she seemed frustrated and pessimistic.

"Sex just isn't satisfying for me," she said, "and there doesn't seem to be anything I can do about it. I want sex less and less, which I think is unfair to Sam. But with his narrow attitudes, I just can't be me. If he were different, I could ask for, you know, some head, and enjoy sex a lot more. But I'm afraid that he just wouldn't accept it if I told him. So I don't say anything."

Gail paused, then continued. "Some days it's easy. But some days I get furious, although I try not to let on. It's especially hard when sex is blah and Sam asks what's the matter. I say nothing, and then I feel a million miles away from him.

"Can you help me enjoy sex more?" she asked. "I feel terribly alone."

As we talked, it became clear that Gail was uncomfortable with any kind of conflict. One of her roles in the marriage, in fact, was steering the two of them away from arguments.

"Especially about sex," she sadly agreed when I raised the point. "Since it's my demands that the fights would be about, it's up to me to keep things calm. I do that by keeping quiet about what I want."

Occasionally, we'd have a session when Gail didn't feel self-critical. She would then feel righteous about her "sacrifice," and how her lack of openness helped keep "harmony" in the marriage. But although she meant well, her strategy wasn't working. Her secrecy and emotional withdrawal weren't solving the problem—they were part of the problem.

After about two months, Gail started to let herself feel the anger that had been accumulating for years. I suggested that she and Sam come in together. Their first joint session started out friendly, but then Sam made a joke about Gail not being all there during sex. That was when she finally exploded.

"I'm not all there because I'm not getting what I want," Gail shouted. "If you were always hiding, you'd have trouble being warm and loving too." The truth was out. Gail paused, then shrugged and told the whole story. Sam was astounded. He hadn't realized Gail was "sacrificing" in the way she described. He certainly had not asked her to.

Sam admitted to Gail that he preferred her to come from intercourse instead of oral sex. "It makes me feel more manly," he said. "But I never realized this whole thing was such a big deal for you. I just want to feel close to you when we have sex together."

The following diagram shows how the isolation resulting from secrecy reinforces itself over time:

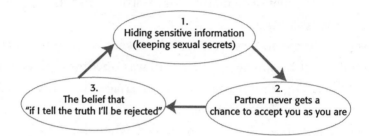

1. Withholding sensitive information . . .
2. prevents your partner from demonstrating his/her love and acceptance, and this . . .
3. perpetuates the belief that telling the truth will lead to rejection, which leads to . . .
1. withholding sensitive information.

Within this classic vicious triangle, isolation takes on a life of its own. That's why choosing to keep a secret is serious business: It separates you from the person you want to feel close to, and makes it difficult to return.

Lowered self-esteem

Low self-esteem is another consequence of secrecy. You've heard of the book for people with poor self-image? It's called "Looking Out for Number 3 or 4."

Imagine finding out that your best friend's mate has never said "I know you and love you exactly the way you are." You'd be sad for both of them, wouldn't you? Yet this is what withholding guarantees: a mate who doesn't know who you really are, who therefore has no chance to *accept* the way you really are.

In most relationships, self-revelation tends to be done on roughly the same level by both parties. When you hesitate to reveal information about yourself, you invite your partner to hesitate as well—even if he or she doesn't know you're withholding. If you keep secrets, therefore, you are far less likely to learn how much your sexuality has in common with that of other people, particularly in the areas you keep secret. In short, secret-keeping makes it harder to know that you're "normal."

Finally, the guilt we usually feel about secrecy also lowers self-esteem. Withholding information from someone we care about breaks an unspoken agreement that most relationships have: We won't keep anything important from each other. In addition, the hiding and secretiveness recall our childhood experiences of sneaking around and breaking rules. Everyone who keeps secrets feels, at times, like a "bad child."

Take another look at how the isolation of secrecy perpetuates itself. You can see how lowered self-esteem fits right into our model:

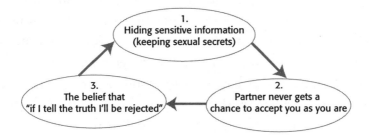

1. Withholding sensitive information. . .
2. prevents your partner from demonstrating his/her love and acceptance. This lowers self-esteem and. . .
3. perpetuates the belief that telling the truth will lead to rejection, which lowers self-esteem and leads to. . .
1. withholding sensitive information.

You probably know that risk-taking is a crucial part of any truly intimate relationship. Unfortunately, both isolation and low self-esteem make risk-taking difficult. If you keep secrets, you probably fear rejection. Performance for its own sake becomes more important than sharing the pleasures of closeness. Real communication is compromised. The delightful process of sharing new parts of yourself is discouraged, which threatens a relationship with going stale.

In Gail's case (and perhaps you can see the same pattern in yourself), isolation and low self-esteem led to uncomfortable feelings such as anger, frustration, and disappointment. It's not unusual to feel betrayed by a lover who you imagine is judging you. If we respect this person, feeling judged lowers our self-worth.

Since such feelings threaten to drag our secrets out into the open, we can only express these feelings indirectly. Ways of acting them out include bullying people; using money to prove our self-worth; and behaving self-destructively, through alcohol abuse, dangerous hobbies, and so on. Constant criticism was the way I expressed anger, disappointment, and isolation in my first marriage many years ago.

These feelings and behaviors actively detract from high self-esteem. Relationships work best with partners who feel good about themselves. That's one reason secrecy makes intimacy difficult.

Sexual problems

Nobody has ever walked into my office and said, "I keep sexual secrets and it's hurting my relationship."

But secrets are a predictable factor in a wide range of sexual problems. Hiding who we are, what we want, how we feel, or what happened in the past prevents us from creating the relaxation, trust, and enthusiasm that satisfying sex requires.

If you are sexually dissatisfied, ask yourself if you're hiding one or more sexual secrets. If so, you may feel anxious about or during sex because:

◇ It threatens to seduce you into letting down your guard, perhaps betraying your secrets.

◇ It's the activity when your partner typically invites closeness, spontaneity, and enthusiasm.

◇ Its very intimacy makes you more vulnerable to your own self-criticism.

Contrary to what you may believe, creating great sex requires very little *doing.* Rather, it involves relaxing, opening the senses, and accepting yourself and your partner.

Secrecy, on the other hand, compels you to hide your body, worry about your performance, fear that your partner is getting bored, or hope that you won't be discovered or rejected. This leaves little attention for how sex actually *feels,* physically or emotionally.

Sexual difficulties come in many forms. They include dysfunctions, such as erection and orgasm problems; impaired, exaggerated, and compulsive desire; medical problems; and lack of enjoyment. Each can be created, maintained, or worsened by withholding information.

Ana, a twenty-nine-year-old dancer, was quite self-confident on a public stage, but very self-conscious in private with her boyfriend Jeff.

COMPLAINT: Lack of orgasm with partner
SECRET: Preferences, turn-ons, and response
FEAR: Being judged; turning off partner

"When I'm alone I have great orgasms," Ana told me. "I know just what to do, and I take plenty of time. But I would never tell my boyfriend I masturbate. Jeff would think he wasn't satisfying me. He's already frustrated that I usually don't come with him."

Since Ana was verbally shy, I suggested she might use her hands or body to communicate with Jeff.

"Show him what to do?" she asked. She rolled her green eyes. "No, I'd be too embarrassed. Besides, if he saw the kind of touching I like, he'd probably think I was weird. Believe me, when I do it alone at home, I'm not very ladylike!

"I wish he would just figure out what to do." She paused. "Well, part of me does. Part of me doesn't, because when I come I really moan and sweat and stuff, and I don't know how he'd react to that." Quietly, Ana added, "I hope you're not going to force me to talk to him about this . . . I really don't want to risk losing him."

Ana knew how to have orgasms. But she didn't feel comfortable sharing the information with her boyfriend. As a result, sex had become a problem that was maintaining distance between them. You can imagine Ana quietly getting angrier and angrier. Over time, her anger, sexual frustration, and pessimism could easily lower her sex drive.

Like most people, Ana hadn't made an explicit decision to hide information about herself; rather, she felt she **had to.** This obligation was based on a fantasy of her boyfriend's reaction, a fantasy that was much more about her than it was about him. She was hoping that hiding the truth would prevent Jeff from judging and leaving her. Ironically, her secrecy was exactly what was pushing them apart.

When she began working with me, Ana couldn't consider the possibility of Jeff accepting her true sexuality. At some point in the relationship, she had simply settled for dissatisfaction. But after twelve sometimes-stormy weeks of therapy, Ana no longer felt like such a bad person. She decided to share her secret with Jeff.

The result? "He was delighted," said a smiling Ana. "He said he'd be willing to try what I liked. And get this—he said he couldn't understand what I had been so afraid of, and why I was so surprised at his reaction!"

Like most people, Jeff was far more open to Ana's secret than she feared he'd be. Her inaccurate assumptions resulted from projecting her negative self-judgment ("My sexuality is bad") onto him ("He'll think my sexuality is bad"). Thus, secrecy helped maintain a painful, unnecessary sexual problem.

Another example concerns an event from the past. I thought this might be so when Sevilla, an attractive mother of twins, started our first session highly concerned about confidentiality.

COMPLAINT: Low desire
SECRET: Previous pregnancy
FEAR: Unwanted pregnancy; being judged a "tramp"

"I don't understand why my sex drive is so low," she said during that first session. She loved her husband, a "good-looking, warm, considerate guy." Telling me about her sexual history, Sevilla hesitated frequently, covering her face with her hand periodically. I had the feeling she was concealing something. When subtle encouragement failed to uncover it, I shared my suspicion with her. Looking at me, Sevilla sighed and plunged ahead.

"I never told my husband about the pregnancy and abortion," she said. "It happened before I met him, and I didn't think it mattered." I looked at her encouragingly and said nothing. "Okay, it would be more honest to say I was afraid of his reaction."

She shrugged. "At first, I didn't want him to think I'd been, y'know, a tramp when I was younger. Eventually, it just became impossible to tell him. For one thing, it never came up; I mean, you don't just casually announce, 'Oh, by the way, six years ago I was pregnant and had an abortion.' "

Contrary to the popular concept of "frigidity," low desire frequently develops in sexually **active** people for whom sex becomes dangerous or painful. Sevilla **wanted** to desire sex more, but fear about being discovered and judged prevented her from thinking about sex as joyful.

I also suspected something else. Did she, like many people who have had unintentional pregnancies, fear another?

"Yes," Sevilla said. "I try not to think about it, but every once in a while I catch myself in the middle of sex thinking, 'What if it happens again?' "

So here was another way in which sex felt dangerous. And because of her commitment to secrecy, Sevilla couldn't really enlist Tito's help in sharing the emotional load.

I told Sevilla that as long as lovemaking reminded her of the past she thought she couldn't reveal, she wouldn't be free to relax and express herself sexually.

"I guess I understand that," she said reluctantly. "And I know Tito will get fed up with this 'not tonight' routine sooner or later."

I agreed. "Eventually, you'll have to do something about this," I said, "even if it only involves reinterpreting your secret for yourself as an acceptable part of the past."

Sevilla's response was grim. "I prefer not to think about the future right now," she said quietly. Sevilla saw me for several more sessions. At that point, she decided not to share her secret with Tito. Not surprisingly, her interest in sex had by then disappeared altogether. Some stories don't have happy endings.

The next story also involves low sexual desire, but in this case, Randy was keeping a secret from himself. It was understandable; knowing his true feelings really were threatening his relationship. Randy's ignorance was costly, however. It was costing him his sex drive.

COMPLAINT: Low desire
SECRET: Does not want a baby
FEAR: Domestic conflict

Randy was the kind of guy people like as soon as they meet him, and I did too. An attractive man, he was well-dressed in a casual, understated way. We made small talk, and then his smiling face darkened.

"I'm really confused about losing interest in sex. Cathy and I used to make love all the time when we were dating, and I enjoyed it a lot. We even got off on the same things, like her blindfolding me. Even now, we only have one small disagreement. She wants a baby more than I do."

That's an interesting clue, I remember thinking. I asked for some details about it. "Actually," said Randy, "she wants a baby right now, and I don't. In two or three years, maybe, but not now, not when we're both so busy with our careers and having so much fun traveling."

I asked if they had had many arguments about the baby issue. "Oh yeah, lots," Randy said, shaking his head. "It used to get pretty bad— Cathy getting depressed, talking about how she's already getting old and that soon it would be too late. I just can't handle her disappointment and all the crying. So we don't talk about it much anymore."

"But not talking about an issue doesn't mean it's gone away," I said.

Randy agreed. "The question is still unresolved, I know," he replied. "It's like a cloud over our lovemaking. Almost every time we do it she looks at me as if to say, 'This is another time that I could be getting pregnant.' "

I asked Randy to look at his hands. To his surprise, he saw that his fists were tightly clenched. Maybe he was angrier than he realized, I suggested. He denied it, but looked thoughtful.

"Sometimes I even worry that she'll forget to take her birth control pills," he continued. "One way or another, I guess this thing is on my mind more than I'd like." He paused. "But what has this all got to do with not wanting to have sex?"

I knew it wouldn't work to confront Randy with a truth he was working so hard to avoid. So, for several weeks, we went slowly. One day "the kid thing," as he called it, came up again.

"Why can't she just wait a year or two?" he asked.

"You know," I replied, "I can imagine you saying that same thing every year for the next ten years."

"If today's mood were permanent, that would be true," he agreed.

"Isn't it?" I inquired.

"It would be, if not for Cathy making me feel bad," he answered. I looked at him, and watched his face suddenly change.

"Do you think" he slowly asked, "that I don't want kids *at all?*" I was silent. "Have I been lying to her?" Randy asked.

"Maybe not so much to her," I gently suggested, "as to yourself."

The realization that Randy didn't want kids at all, didn't resolve the marital problems right away. In fact, things became rougher for a while. But just acknowledging the truth made Randy feel much better—"as if I can breathe again," as he put it—and his sex drive began to return. Then he and Cathy were able to start talking about their future in a more productive, adult way, which may include ending the marriage.

Randy's story illustrates an important principle: When the consequences of sexual honesty are frightening, sex often loses its appeal.

Frequently, other forms of intimacy become more difficult as well. Many secret-keepers are afraid of losing a relationship all at once. Instead, they lose it over time, piece by piece.

Joseph's story shows how secrecy can result in the need to control sexual interactions tightly. This dynamic made good sex extremely difficult for this soft-spoken security guard.

COMPLAINT: Frequent lack of erection
SECRET: Intense, "abnormal" fantasies
FEAR: Losing control, offending partner

"One of my favorite things during sex," Joseph told me in his second session, "is to imagine I'm with someone else. Sometimes I fantasize that I'm forcing someone to have sex, or that there's another girl there with us. Or that someone is watching us through the window, or listening to us."

Joseph paused, looking at me. I think he wanted to see if I was disgusted or shocked. Clearly, I was neither. I wasn't sure if he was pleased or disappointed.

"Basically, I have a lot of thoughts during sex that are, well, not normal, you see? Being impotent on top of that really makes sex a problem," he said. "See, mentally I'm going a hundred miles an hour, and in bed I'm just a zero."

"I don't imagine that you've shared these fantasies with your partners," I said. "Of course not," he replied. But how about sharing his concerns **about** his thoughts, rather than the thoughts themselves—could he do that? "No, I wouldn't dare tell my lady friends about this," he said. "They'd run in the opposite direction, don't you think?"

Joseph's fear of his own sexuality unconsciously interfered with his erection. Sex had to be a carefully controlled activity, lest someone discover the "real" Joseph, who was "raunchy" and "perverse." Under such circumstances, it would feel dangerous to be comfortable during sex.

Joseph needed to know just how common his fantasies were. During our time together, we discussed the possible value of joining a men's group, talking to friends, or reading popular self-help books like Bernie Zilbergeld's *Male Sexuality*, Shere Hite's *Report on Male Sexuality*, or Levine and Barbach's *The Intimate Male*.

Joseph desperately needed to realize that he was "normal." At that point he could **decide** whether or not he wanted to discuss his fantasies and experiences with a partner. Regardless of his choices, the perspective of "normalcy" would help Joseph regain a sense of calmness and safety about sex. That would be a crucial step toward having dependable erections. The jackpot would be for Joseph to decide to add a new dimension to what he wants in a woman: "someone I feel comfortable talking to."

When our work ended, that was exactly how Joseph described the "ideal mate" he was now looking for. I believe he'll find her, too.

Ted's story is about masturbation. It's particularly poignant to me because I hear it so frequently—and because it involves so much needless suffering.

COMPLAINT: Rapid ejaculation
SECRET: Masturbation
FEAR: Making partner feel inadequate; being judged "immature"

Ted was a veteran firefighter with large, callused hands and a thick black mustache. His best friend had been in marriage counseling with me the previous year, "So you come highly recommended," he said. "But I have to tell you, I'm skeptical about shrinks. I want to be honest about that from the beginning."

"Anyway, the story is, I masturbated as a kid. We all did, right?" he began. "Well, one of my buddies got caught one time, and his grand-mother almost killed him."

I've heard this story hundreds of times from both men and women. On this day it reminded me of Truman Capote's great line: "The one great advantage of masturbation is that you don't have to dress up for it."

Ted's voice snapped me back to his story. "Bobby's grandma told him he'd get terrible pimples, and that his dick would fall off. Bobby told me what happened, and we laughed about it for months afterwards. But when our faces broke out a year later we were petrified! We both tried to swear off, but it didn't work. How do you stop doing something that feels so good?"

"Well, now I'm married," he continued. "I love my wife and the sex is fine, but once or twice a week I like to sneak off alone and give myself a good hand job. But it's just like when I was a kid—in the bathroom, pretending to be doing something else. And definitely not taking my time. I usually have to do it pretty quickly."

That Ted felt obliged to keep his secret was not unusual. "I know if my wife found out, she'd feel real bad, like she wasn't satisfying me. It would almost be like I was being unfaithful. So I don't say anything."

Ted was suffering under a double burden. Unintentionally, he had trained himself to climax quickly. His hurried style of masturbation had been transferred to his lovemaking. In addition, his guilt was prevent-ing him from relaxing and enjoying intercourse. This anxiety was also triggering the rapid ejaculation.

Ted's secrecy, of course, prevented his wife from accepting his inter-est, from reducing his guilt, and from giving him a chance to retrain himself to make love in a more relaxed way. It also rescued her from hav-ing to grow in the relationship. Anxiety was an inevitable product of the secrecy—not of the masturbation, but of the secrecy around it.

Still haunted by his early scares about masturbation, Ted was, metaphorically, stuck in childhood. He was still dealing with the profound message that his sexuality is bad. Reversing this heritage and accepting his normalcy would be the first step toward improving Ted's sexual functioning.

Incidentally, Ted could do this with or without his wife's support. Sharing the secret with her is not nearly as important as accepting it himself.

Old emotional wounds

Millions of people have been traumatized through incest, childhood exploitation, rape, or coerced sex while dating. In the past, our lack of understanding led us to underestimate the frequency and impact of such events. In many cases we even blamed the victim. You can understand why most people have felt obliged to keep such events secret.

These traumatic incidents almost always involve secrecy. The wrongdoer says, "Don't tell your mother," or "Don't tell the police," or "If you tell my friends, I'll deny it." Most victims maintain the secrecy later as adults. This is a terrible, painful repetition of the original victimization. This time, ironically, it is perpetuated by the victims themselves.

If trust and intimacy are to flourish in a relationship, sexually traumatic experiences must somehow be resolved. This is difficult under the best of circumstances. Self-imposed silence makes it even harder.

Withholding prevents you from sharing the healing energy of your loved ones. Although some partners deal with their own pain by either blaming the victim or not believing the story, it is more likely that your partner will be supportive. Continued secrecy robs you of the chance to be accepted as you really are. It helps maintain your belief that there is something wrong with you because you were exploited.

The belief that concealment is mandatory keeps you living in the past—acting like a victim still being coerced. Speaking out and seizing the **choice** of how to run your life—including whether, and whom to tell—ends the victim role for good.

That's the point about Theresa, a woman with vaginismis (involuntary spasm of the vaginal muscles). She was almost in tears when she came to me about the problem. "We have a good marriage except for one thing," said the young school teacher. "Whenever we try to have intercourse, my vagina just clamps shut.

"At first, Roberto was patient," she sniffled, "but eventually we both became irritable and fought about it a lot. Doctors mostly gave me simple advice that didn't work, like have a glass of wine at bedtime to relax."

Eventually, one physician sent her to me for sex therapy. He had examined her and found no physical pathology. Suspecting that Theresa's problem was caused by a very bad sexual experience in the past, I gently suggested that such a connection was not uncommon. She quickly changed the subject, which I allowed without comment.

Then, near the end of the session, she brought it up herself. "I never told anyone about it, because I was ashamed," she said. "I certainly couldn't tell Roberto—I was afraid he'd kill my father. I just figured I had to live with it." The truth was out: As a young girl, Theresa had been sexually exploited by her father.

The following week, we discussed her family background, including the sexual abuse. We talked about various ways of exploring its effects. Theresa decided to join a group for women. She agreed to come in again after her first group meeting.

The following week, she told me all about the meeting, amazed at how many other women had stories just like hers. Feeling encouraged, she continued seeing me and attending the group. "Those people have made me feel normal and accepted for the first time in years," she said at one point.

About a month later, she said that several of the women had encouraged her to tell Roberto. "They say I won't feel so alone, that it will bring us closer. What do you think?" she asked.

We discussed it for several months. Finally, she made her decision. "I know you believe my sex problem is connected to the thing with my father. If that's true," she said steadily, "I don't think my marriage can afford my not talking about it anymore."

Theresa was scared, but she worked up the courage to tell her husband. The next day she came in ready to burst. "It was just like I figured it would be," she cried. "He yelled a lot, said crazy things. He wanted to run right out and kill my father," she sobbed.

At that point I asked to see Theresa and Roberto together. Although they clearly loved each other, the session was filled with accusations and tears. For weeks, there were late-night phone calls between us. But eventually the power of their love triumphed. Roberto began to accept what had happened in the past, which allowed Theresa to finish accepting it herself.

"I've decided not to confront my father about this," Theresa told me one week. "I feel done." By the end of the session, I agreed with her. That's when I assigned her a series of exercises to do at home. Sex gradually became easier, and about three months later she and Roberto were having enjoyable intercourse together.

Theresa's case is a vivid example of how secrecy can keep us imprisoned in the past. Finally speaking honestly about her trauma enabled Theresa to separate the dangerous past from the safe present. Her vaginal spasms went away soon after; they were no longer needed as protection from unwanted invasion.

The illusion—and its price

Sexual secrecy does appear to make the world of relationships safer (at virtually no cost), but this sense of safety is an illusion. Since the threat of literal annihilation is actually in the past, there is nothing you can do in the present to make you safer back then.

The illusion of safety carries a high price tag. Although withholding cannot change the childhood experiences that felt so threatening, the results of pursuing childhood safety through adult secrecy does have powerful, unintended effects. The sense you get isn't real power; it's *pseudo-power.* That is, you give up the drive to be accepted as okay—and instead, you settle for not being attacked (by yourself or by others) for not being okay.

Maurice (who we met earlier) gave up on the possibility of being accepted as okay, supposedly because he had herpes. Instead, he settled for not being attacked or rejected because of his herpes. He did this by hiding the condition.

Strategies that tap pseudo-power often involve withholding: for example, not telling a partner how you like to be stimulated, or what turns you off. A *truly* powerful approach is taking the initiative: "I'd like us to make my orgasm more of a priority. How could we do that?"

Withholding information also seems valuable as a way of creating and controlling emotional distance in relationships. Once we restrict closeness, however, we generally have difficulty making it flourish fully again. Intimacy is the product of trust, of the willingness to risk and explore *with* another person. Once one partner asserts control over the process, it stops being mutual. Closeness may not grow any further until circumstances change.

Acting out feelings through sexual secrecy can provide temporary psychological comfort. But it also keeps you from communicating effectively, and from having the kind of power you need to change a painful situation. This is the problem with acting out survival fears: You feel better in the short run but guarantee that you'll feel bad again soon. Ironically, by hiding the truth or concealing the past we create the very situations we most fear.

Some relationships, unfortunately, discourage the direct expressions of feelings. There are marriages that need a weak or frightened spouse in order to be stable. Beliefs like "I can't make it on my own" help these relationships last, but they stunt the growth of the participants.

In such cases, rebellion—through sexual secrecy—is a way for the partner who plays the weak and frightened role to act out anger and shame. Unfortunately, you can be so caught up in survival issues that you fail to see their disastrous long-term effects.

Finally, using sexual secrecy to fulfill childhood scripts is very costly. As we discussed earlier, character scripts emerge as the mind grapples with a single goal: preventing childhood pain. So our old scripts specifically ignore our contemporary, adult needs.

Such scripts are like an aunt who wants to protect her niece from rowdy boys who are only interested in "one thing." The trouble is, the niece is now thirty, and wants to meet a nice guy. If she listens to her aunt, she never will. As with acting out, the problem with slavishly following a lifelong script is that it feels good in the moment, but prevents happiness in the long run.

Looking at the many illusions surrounding sexual secrecy, and their costs, is a crucial step toward improving your sexual satisfaction and sexual relationships. Almost anyone willing to do this will be rewarded by deeper, more intimate relationships and richer, more satisfying sexual experiences, whether casual or committed.

Given the unconscious fear many of us have about sexuality and relationships, secrecy looks like an attractive way to avoid the judgments and unpredictable attacks we anticipate from those we allow close to us. And so we experience the advantages of secrecy. It is a way of acting out feelings that otherwise seem dangerous, of creating distance, of seizing what *feels* like power but really isn't, and of fulfilling old, outdated psychological scripts.

Silence makes relationships seem safer by reducing the amount of trust and commitment we need in order to participate in them. It lets us create a private world within our relationships, allowing us to avoid our own uncomfortable feelings.

Unexamined, the costs of these wonderful advantages seem low. This is especially true if you work them into your personality, reinforcing whatever tendencies you have toward being dour, flighty, snide, resigned, and so on. The truth, of course, is that the costs are high. But given the dilemma we humans find ourselves in—needing other people in order to survive, and fearing that this need will destroy us—this is a difficult truth to hear.

Perhaps more to the point, it's difficult to tell a man who is sure he's being chased that his getaway car has a tire that's about to blow out.

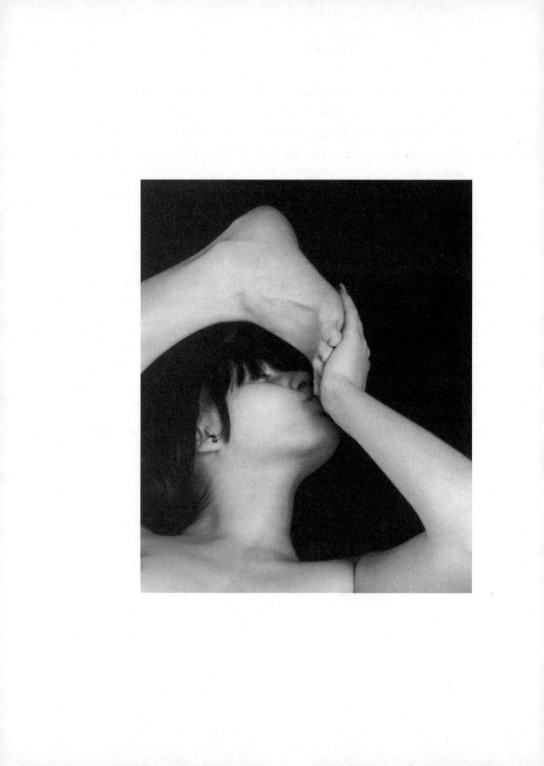

Chapter 4

Sexual Secrets:
Arousal and Response

⊚⊚

There may be some things that are better than sex, and there may be some things worse. But there's nothing exactly like it.

—W. C. FIELDS

There is an Indian fable I like very much: There once was a man who was so displeased by the sight of his own shadow that he determined to be rid of it forever. He commenced to run, but no matter how fast he went, he could not get away from it. So he ran, faster and faster. Finally, the constant running so exhausted the man that he dropped dead.

He did not realize that if only he had stopped running and had sat down under a tree, his shadow would have disappeared.

Jack is a thirty-nine-year-old machinist who put a lot of energy into protecting himself and his community from "sexual perversion." Jack was against school sex education because he felt it encouraged kids to have sex. He wanted gays jailed or "cured" so they couldn't seduce "straights." He tried to stop the private rental of X-rated videos because they "promoted sick ideas" about lovemaking. And he believed only married couples should have access to contraception.

Jack's deep wish to restrict other people's sexual expression was really a statement about himself. He was clearly afraid of the power of sexuality—particularly his own. To deal with his fear he had, unconsciously, made this potentially dangerous sexuality into an external object. Because this "object" came from within himself, he saw the danger everywhere. He acted as if it were a contagious disease, and that he was especially vulnerable.

A powerful interest in sexuality was Jack's secret, which he hid even from himself. Rather than become aware of his fear, confront it, and deal with it, he became attached to distorted theories about sex and its expression. He felt safest in groups of people who agreed with him, where others loudly denied **their** powerful sexuality, too. Together they joined forces to destroy the sexual enemy "out there."

I didn't try to talk Jack out of his opinions. Instead, I helped him become aware of the unconscious belief that a vital part of him was bad. Until he changed that belief, he would see the devil lurking everywhere. You can't, after all, run away from your shadow.

What is "proper" sexual conduct?

By the time we are adults, the Secrecy Imperative has taken its toll. We think of our incestuous fantasies, our curiosity about other bodies, our joyful desire to masturbate, and the rest of our sexuality as shameful, needing to be controlled.

In an attempt to protect ourselves from this "bad" part, we unconsciously reject it or split it off from the rest of our psyche. This is the opposite of the wholeness and self-acceptance that define mental health. Although it is painful to disown any part of ourselves, it usually feels absolutely necessary. "If you don't control that nasty sexuality," says your inner voice, "it will control you."

That's why we will do virtually anything to protect ourselves from this "bad" part. We will even sacrifice our self-respect, or live without intimacy.

Gaining distance from your "dangerous" sexuality is not something you can do once and forget about it; it's a lifelong job. You may briefly succeed in chasing away sexual thoughts and feelings, but they will always be on the brink of pushing their way back into your awareness. For someone who is sure that these sexual images are bad, round-the-clock mental vigilance is crucial.

One way to exercise this discipline is by following the social norms that define acceptable sexual behavior. In effect, we mentally chaperone ourselves. Adjectives such as "polite," "ladylike," "respectable," and "normal" describe such behavior. All other kinds of sex, such as non-marital, nonintercourse, or nonreproductive are denigrated as dirty, animal-like, unnatural, or sinful. Familiar cultural definitions of "normal" sexual conduct include:

- ◇ Penis-vagina intercourse, missionary position.
- ◇ Between one male and one female, who love each other.
- ◇ Initiated by him.
- ◇ He has an instant, firm erection.
- ◇ She is ladylike (not too sweaty, noisy, or enthusiastic).
- ◇ She lubricates copiously.
- ◇ Sex is simple and does not require any discussion.
- ◇ She comes easily.
- ◇ He doesn't come until after she does.

According to various surveys, however, most of us don't fit this mold of "proper" arousal and response. Recent university, magazine, and foundation surveys all report that oral sex is almost as common as intercourse, and that millions of Americans enjoy anal sex.

Sad to say, many of us feel compelled to withhold information about our preferences from our partners or from ourselves. Why? Because we fear we'll be rejected for enjoying sex the "wrong way." It's a dreadful reminder from childhood. In this adult version, our partner is the parent and we become the child. Thus, the childhood strategy seems safest: When in doubt, hide the truth.

Unfortunately, this is going to leave you feeling guilty, fearing discovery, and knowing you're not loved for your true self. So publicly, we profess the faith of "straight" sex. But people do quite varied things. Hence, the old saying: "What I like is variety. What you like is kinky. What they like is perverse."

For example, few of us are willing to say that erotic films and books should **not** be suppressed; no one wants to be accused of favoring pornography. And yet, erotica is a multi-billion-dollar industry. It simply couldn't exist with only a few thousand demented customers. Tens of millions of normal people consume erotica every year.

Adult bookstore owners have been saying for years that their customers are you and me. But, fearing punishment, no one wants to admit it. Most of us aren't adult enough to seize the power to make our own sexual judgments and decisions. We're still masturbating in the bathroom, hiding from Mommy.

The sources of secrecy

Let's look at some common sexual secrets about arousal and response: what turns us on, and how we react to being turned on, including preferences, conditions, sex drive, body image, sexual dysfunction, and "You don't really turn me on."

PREFERENCES

One of the most prevalent sources of secrecy involves the kinds of sexual stimulation we like. In a culture that defines the "right way" so narrowly, it isn't surprising that so many common preferences are considered deviant. Just what we need—another reason to feel ashamed about our sexuality.

For example, more than half of American women say they need clitoral, not vaginal, stimulation for climaxing, according to studies by Shere Hite and Lonnie Barbach. Yet many men and women, misled by romance literature, Freudian psychology, and traditional folk wisdom, find this common preference strange or undesirable.

How exasperating is this cultural bias? Barbach notes in her lectures that, "Women are as frustrated by this as men would be if they believed they were supposed to reach orgasm by having their testicles rubbed."

Because intercourse doesn't usually provide enough clitoral stimulation, many women prefer oral or manual sex so they can come. Some men prefer making love this way too, because it requires less energy, produces more intense sensations, and involves less performance pressure. Yet, many men and women keep quiet about this and other preferences.

Elliot a healthy, middle-aged man who enjoyed sex, did just that. He functioned just fine, but his preference for fellatio over intercourse troubled him. His worry led him to seek treatment.

"Perhaps deep down, I'm gay," he said anxiously during our first session. "God, I hope not. I certainly don't want anyone else to think that. Besides, how do you know that a woman isn't resenting giving a blow job, but doing it anyway?" Understandably, Elliot never asked his dates to go down on him. And he hesitated to accept a woman doing it spontaneously. Periodically, he'd stop dating altogether. Sexuality became a lonely conflict between pleasure, frustration, and worry.

After two sessions, it was clear that Elliot didn't have any special problems with intimacy. What he needed most was reassurance that he was normal. I thought the *Hite Report* would help. It states that: "Almost all [of the 7,000 interviewed] men said that they enjoyed fellatio tremendously."

I suggested Elliot ask a few women friends how they felt about it. Three of the four he asked assured him that they enjoyed it. He now believes that his interest is "normal," that he can trust himself, and that he no longer needs to be secretive about his preferences. Elliot is now working on accepting his sexuality regardless of how common his preferences are, or aren't. As long as he and his partners are comfortable and satisfied, Elliot has the option of assuming his sexuality is okay.

Women are faced with this dilemma as frequently as men. A thirty-year-old caterer named Keneesha was referred to me by her physician. Keneesha was worried because she preferred hand or mouth stimulation of her clitoris far more than other forms of sex.

Keneesha had intercourse mostly to please her husband, Don. Although she enjoyed the closeness, she usually felt frustrated afterward. She encouraged Don to "do more," but she couldn't "admit" her need. Without an explicit discussion, they couldn't get in sync.

What troubled Keneesha most was sneaking away to the bathroom after intercourse to masturbate. Because she was usually very aroused, orgasm took only a minute. But the pleasure was mixed with other feelings: anger at her husband for not satisfying her, guilt about needing a hand job and having one without him, and fear that he would find out and feel rejected.

After only two therapy sessions, Keneesha decided to "come out" to Don. As she told me a few days later, "It was just as bad as I feared. He was insulted and we fought bitterly."

In the weeks that followed, Keneesha and Don argued about sex often. They blamed each other, dug up old wounds, and accused each other of being inadequate. "But finally I realized that I'd had enough," she told me one day. "I did some soul-searching. I asked Don, 'Aren't I still the same loving wife that I've always been? I have a simple sexual need, and I won't apologize for it.'"

That's when Keneesha and Don started marital counseling. It was clear they had more than a sexual problem, they had a power problem. Keneesha's honesty had forced it into the open, and there would be no going back. She and Don are still having rough times, but their conflicts have changed. They have more respect for each other and are aiming for a new kind of honesty. If they can attain this honesty, they'll be closer than before.

CONDITIONS

As therapist Bernie Zilbergeld noted in his classic book, *Male Sexuality*, each of us has unique, individual conditions for satisfying sex. Despite what we've learned from romance novels and James Bond films, simply having a willing partner is not enough. Yet many people believe that when it comes to sexual desire and satisfaction, men should be like ATMs—readily available and operating twenty-four hours a day.

In real life, the variety of requirements for enjoyable sex is almost endless. Examples include privacy, closeness, a youthful partner, a sense of rule-breaking, and reliable contraception.

"A condition," Zilbergeld wrote, is "anything that makes you more relaxed, comfortable, confident, and open to your sexual experience." It's something that helps "clear your nervous system of unnecessary clutter, leaving it open to receive and transmit sexual messages" in satisfying ways. "When sex doesn't work out the way we like, we are too ready to assume that something is wrong with us, rather than with the situation."

Believing we shouldn't have conditions, we hide them. Conditions are another aspect of sexuality that many of us keep secret or try to ignore. Some conditions involve particular turn-offs. For different people, these might include being teased about their body shape or weight, a sense of being rushed, the smell of cigarettes, a partner's mechanical technique. One of my own conditions—I admit it—is *no* country music.

Since sex without our conditions can be scary, boring, frustrating, or unpleasant, why do we so often agree to have sex without them? Usually because we don't believe others will accept our conditions—because we don't accept them ourselves. The issue makes me think of Simon, a small business owner I worked with a few years ago.

"I'm crazy about this new girl," he told me. "She's very pretty, and she likes me." So why, he asked, was he losing interest in their lovemaking?

I asked if there were any problems outside of bed. "Oh, she likes to drink," he replied. "In fact, she likes me to drink, too. Says it makes her feel sexy." And how did he feel about it? "Oh, I don't love it," he said, "but it's okay, I guess." It was one of those answers that rings a bell in a therapist's mind; I decided to hang on to it for the time being.

The following week Simon was back. "We made love again," he said as soon as he sat down. "And halfway through, the same damn thing happened. What's wrong with me?"

I asked Simon to close his eyes and visualize the situation. What did he hear, smell, feel, and taste?

"Gloria's skin," he smiled. "It feels so soft. And music. We both like cello music. Now she's whispering to me." I saw him wrinkle his nose. "Anything wrong?" I asked. "No," he said quickly, but under his breath I heard something. "What is it?" I asked again.

"Just the booze," he said, with a trace of anger. "Why does she have to spoil it with the booze?" It was clear that Simon hated the smell of alcohol on Gloria's breath. He said he had mentioned it to her once or twice, had gotten no response, and had dropped it.

During our session, Simon realized that he disliked Gloria smelling of alcohol partly because it reminded him of his childhood, when he was cared for by an inept, alcoholic grandfather. Rather than confront Gloria, however, Simon decided to swallow his discomfort.

"I'm the one who should change," he said, stoically. "This is a stupid thing to get upset about. Besides," he added quietly, "what if she refuses to change?"

This, of course, was what the withholding was about. Simon chose to stay on the very difficult path of denying, and therefore hiding, one of his most important conditions. His resentment showed itself, indirectly, in his wavering libido. I think larger problems lie ahead for him.

Concern about the reasonableness of a condition is just another version of the most widespread sexual concern: "Am I normal?"

SEX DRIVE

Many people deny the true nature of their sex drive, believing themselves abnormal. According to Shere Hite, "There is a great deal of anxiety on the part of most men [surveyed] about how often they have intercourse." In fact, "Many men are fairly sure that they should be having it more often than they are."

Since men are supposed to want sex more than women, they frequently hide what they consider a too-low desire. They may even initiate sex when they don't really want it. Instead of just politely refusing their partner's invitation, some men will pick a fight, or say they're tired, or get involved in TV or reading, or wait until their partner is asleep before going to bed. As a long-term, unconscious solution, these men often get a second job, adopt new civic responsibilities, or acquire a new hobby.

Women, on the other hand, more often hide a too-high desire. They may try therapy to get "fixed," or masturbate in an attempt to decrease their interest, or experiment with lingerie, perfume, cosmetics, diets, even plastic surgery, to get their partner interested. How different these women's lives would be if they simply admitted the truth about their sex drive and worked with their mates to find a reasonable resolution.

This reminds me of when I was the guest on a call-in radio show, and a listener asked me to define "nymphomaniac." "Sexual labels are arbitrary and relative," I told him. "Many people think that a nymphomaniac is any woman who wants sex one more time than her partner."

You may be hiding or repressing your true sex drive out of fear of rejection, but there is often another reason. You may be someone who is convinced that your sexuality is bad, who fears that "giving in" to it will allow it to take over, and overpowered by lust, you'll want sex all the time. A woman referred to me by a social worker turned out to fit this description.

Rachel had an extremely low sexual drive. "I love my husband," she said, "but I just don't want sex with him very much." The problem had started a year earlier after a long vacation during which they had made love every day. What was it about the intense pleasure, I wondered, that had dampened her pilot light?

Eventually, we started discussing her adolescence. "My parents were workaholics, with very little time for me," she recalled. "They didn't care much about my schoolwork or friends or anything. At fifteen I went all the way with a college guy I was dating. The ecstatic look on his face when he came thrilled me. When he said he loved me I just melted.

"That year, I slept with most of his friends," she continued. "I became hooked on this new drug of making men go wild, and I developed quite a reputation. But by the time I was twenty I felt old. I began to realize that these guys didn't care about me, that they had just used me. In my own way, I suppose, I had used them too. A year later, I met Lee, the first decent guy I ever knew. I married him as fast as I could, and then we left the state."

Unconsciously, Rachel believed that this five-year period of intense sexual activity was her true nature. She had spent the years since fearing that the "madness" of uncontrolled sexual interest would return, get hold of her, and ruin her life. Feeling safe in her new marriage, she was slowly working out a satisfying sexual arrangement with Lee—until the second honeymoon.

I asked if Lee knew about the "wild days." Some, she replied quietly, but not much. She was afraid that if he found out he'd be upset. "I don't like to think about it. That would almost be like inviting it all back," she said.

Here, then, was the secret: "I've been bad." And the fear? "I'm afraid Lee will judge me and then leave me." The intense sexual activity on their vacation had restimulated all the old fears about getting out of control. Her subsequent loss of desire was an unconscious way of coping with those fears.

I gently encouraged Rachel to accept the way she had handled a difficult childhood. Some teens, I told her, develop problems with alcohol, theft, or school as coping mechanisms to compensate for the lack of parental attention. Sex had been her ingenious, if unintentional, solution.

Once Rachel began to accept that she wasn't bad, she became less afraid that Lee would judge her. More importantly, she became less afraid of losing control of her sexuality. Eventually she decided to ask Lee to come in with her for a joint session so she could share her fears with him. Today, Rachel enjoys sex in an exciting, intimate relationship with her husband.

BODY IMAGE

In some ways, body features are the most universally kept sexual secrets. All of us, particularly women, have moments when we want to hide our bodies. Yet few of us are able to talk about this and grow beyond it.

Much of the problem stems from our culture's obsession with physical beauty. We may spend more time improving our body's appearance than we spend improving our minds or our health. Not surprisingly, some Americans develop disorders such as anorexia and bulimia, in which distorted self-image leads to dangerous self-starvation.

Predictably, Americans are also in love with plastic surgery. This multi-billion-dollar industry offers dozens of procedures, including breast enlargement, tummy tucks, chemical peels, collagen injections, liposuction, and face lifts, which are often painful and sometimes disastrous.

The shame we feel about our bodies is probably most acute before or during sexual encounters. We may be embarrassed about scars, too little or too much hair, or what we believe are ugly genitalia. Almost half the email my website receives expresses concern about genital size or shape. And according to the women I hear from, breasts come in only two sizes: too large and too small.

According to a recent study, the single factor most responsible for whatever sexual inhibitions today's women feel is insecurity about physical appearance. Fully 41 percent [of 26,000 respondents] said that these feelings prevent them from freely expressing their sexuality.

Shame about our bodies drains our energy and creativity. People who keep such secrets often want the lights off during sex, and may refuse to make love in positions they feel are unflattering, even if enjoyable. Sometimes they prohibit certain kinds of touching that might reveal their imperfections.

A secret can be almost anything: a scar, asymmetrical breasts, a hairy backside, inverted nipples, small testicles. Our tendency to feel ashamed of normal variations in body features is quite impressive. And quite unfortunate.

Sandy is an intelligent, vivacious woman who is about thirty pounds overweight. She came to me because she had trouble reaching orgasm with a partner. I asked about a typical sexual encounter.

"First of all, I won't get on top, even though it's really my favorite position. I don't want anyone seeing how much my breasts sag. Other positions are out, too—doing it from behind, for example, because my butt is huge and I know any guy would be turned off.

"Once I decide to make love with someone, I suggest my house. I keep lots of candles by the bed, so the lighting is soft, more flattering. I discourage men from touching my belly or thighs. It feels good to *me*, but they're, you know, squishy, flabby. It's just too embarrassing.

"Although I feel okay about the whole thing most of the time," Sandy continued, "sometimes I feel like a second-class citizen. I get angry at men for being so prejudiced, and then I get angry at myself for caring so much. And of course, it's frustrating to get excited and then not come. Sometimes I worry that this turns men off too. What the hell, when it's too much I just stop dating for a few months. Then I forget the bad feelings, and I get back into it."

Although Sandy likes sex, a big part of lovemaking involves monitoring her body's attractiveness. Her attention is divided between trying to enjoy sex and trying to hide her body. The conflict between these activities made orgasm difficult for her, while her rules about touching prevented the stimulation she needed. No wonder she couldn't come with a partner.

Sandy's anger about feeling lonely and demeaned is yet another obstacle to satisfaction. And it's understandable; Sandy feels out of control. Her secrecy, which dictates her behavior, has rendered her powerless.

This reminds me of the shy couple who made love only during total eclipses of the sun. That's because they wouldn't take their clothes off unless it was dark everywhere in the world.

Other information about our bodies that is sometimes omitted includes:

◇ I'm sterile (and I know you want children, so I'm not going to tell you right now).
◇ I have herpes or some other STD (and although it's under control right now, I'm afraid you would reject me if I told you).
◇ I'm a woman who comes very easily, and/or has multiple orgasms (and I'm afraid you'd be intimidated or judgmental if you knew).
◇ I'm afraid to make love without a few drinks first.

SEXUAL DYSFUNCTION

According to pioneering sexologists Masters and Johnson, at least 40 million Americans are sexually dissatisfied. Ideally, such a widespread problem would be freely discussed, but it isn't so. On the contrary, having a sexual problem or concern is one of the most common sexual secrets.

Sexual dysfunction carries a sort of moral blemish, the way alcoholism and divorce used to (and still do in some places). Thus, we often choose to hide a sexual problem from our partners, from professionals who might help us, and through denial, rationalization, and projection, even from ourselves.

Forty-four-year-old William was a teamster with such a dilemma. "About a year ago I lost my hard-on in the middle of lovemaking, for the first time. It didn't bother me that much, but when it happened again the next night, I got nervous," he told me.

"Both of my main girlfriends were leaving town to take better jobs about then, so I was soon back in circulation, as they say. In the first few months I met a couple of new women, so I was back in business. But I had the impotence a couple more times, and that did it. No more lovemaking, I decided, until I get this fixed."

I pondered the probability that his girlfriends' departure helped cause the original erectile problem, but I said nothing. I wanted to hear the story William's way, without interruption.

William fidgeted a bit and went on. "I became pretty creative at excuses: Early day with my kid tomorrow; too much to drink; got a lot on my mind; too upset by the movie we just saw. It was lonely, but better than admitting I had a sex problem.

"I've seen a few doctors," he concluded, "but they can't seem to fix me. I'm pretty discouraged right now. And, of course, I don't feel I can hold on to a woman indefinitely without sex."

William's situation reminded me of the difference between anxiety and panic. Anxiety is what you feel the first time you can't get an erection twice. Panic is what you feel the second time you can't get an erection once. William had only been anxious for a few days when he went straight to panic.

Like most of us, William could manage a long time without intercourse. But the lack of touching and affection troubled him a great deal. He also felt very bad about fooling the women he dated.

His guilt combined with his constant monitoring of potentially "dangerous" situations kept William from making emotional contact with his girlfriends. Sadly, his feelings prevented him from discovering that there were women who would have accepted him just as he *was*. Sharing this information would have been a calculated risk, but it could have resulted in the nurturing William needed so badly.

JUDGEMENTS AND CRITICISM

A surprisingly large number of people are highly critical of the way their partners make love. Judgements may include:

- ✧ "You don't really turn me on."
- ✧ "You're lousy in bed."
- ✧ "I don't like what we do."
- ✧ "I'm bored with your lack of creativity."
- ✧ "You never initiate sex."

In a way, criticisms like these are the ultimate sexual secret. Since it intimately involves your mate's self-concept, sharing truly tests a relationship.

And yet, concealing sexual judgments prevails. Shere Hite reports that many men wish their partners would go down on them differently, but say nothing. Dozens of writers, including Anaïs Nin, attest to women's reluctance to discuss the way their partners make love.

Perhaps you hide your dissatisfaction secret because:

- ✧ You're not supposed to know what good sex is.
- ✧ You don't want to upset your partner.
- ✧ You're not sure you deserve good sex.
- ✧ You don't believe that sex can be satisfying or comfortable.
- ✧ It lets you hold onto the fantasy that things will somehow change in the future.

Akiko and Claude were an affluent couple in their late thirties who obviously loved each other. They appeared to "have it all"—money, careers, a beautiful child. But they just couldn't seem to find time for lovemaking. He had an important corporate position, and he also supervised the maid and gardener. She had a busy law practice, was raising their child, and performed in a local orchestra.

Interestingly, they both agreed that Claude was the sex expert in the marriage. "He's had lots of experience," said Akiko. Claude obviously enjoyed this respect.

In private, however, Akiko added some interesting detail. She was not really satisfied with Claude's lovemaking. "But I can't criticize it," she explained. "He knows a lot more about sex than I do. I just need to get with it a little more. I'll get the hang of it eventually."

I asked her to visualize a perfect sexual encounter with a stranger: the pace, activities, and feelings. The scene she described was quite different from her routine with Claude. When I pointed this out, Akiko became thoughtful. Then she understood. "It's not up to me to fit in with his 'expertise,' " she suddenly exclaimed, "It's up to him to do what I like!"

Which meant, of course, that she would have to explain her dissatisfaction and desire for change. This meant dethroning Claude as the expert, and establishing herself as a co-expert. Akiko was understandably hesitant because doing so would definitely change the balance of power in the rest of her marriage. But she decided to tell the truth so she could enjoy sex more and feel closer to Claude. It wasn't easy, but it worked.

Akiko understands the dynamics fairly well. She is still, however, hesitant to act. Which is probably how most of us feel about the secrets described in this chapter. After all, the more closely we identify with one of our secrets, the more we hesitate to reveal it. And it's difficult to imagine anything that could be more individual, more "us," than our arousal and response pattern.

In the next chapter, we'll look at fantasies and feelings.

Chapter 5

Sexual Secrets:
Fantasies and Feelings

❡❡

The conscious mind allows itself to be trained like a parrot, but the unconscious mind does not—which is why St. Augustine thanked God for not making him responsible for his dreams.

—CARL JUNG

A favorite teacher of mine once remarked, "Anyone without feelings or fantasies can safely be declared dead." Certainly, we humans typically have a high volume of images running around in our heads at any given time.

People have sexual feelings and fantasies for many reasons. A routine week for most of us includes a great deal of sexual stimulation from films and TV, advertising, romance novels, and suggestive and revealing clothing. Most work, residential, and recreational environments mix the two genders, frequently providing close physical contact.

Sexual anxieties are common primarily because of the cultural belief that there are correct ways to think and feel sexually. This belief implies, of course, that some ways are wrong or inadequate. The media tend to suggest that anyone who is sexually frustrated is, indeed, doing or feeling something wrong.

In fact, the media consciously encourage the feeling of sexual inadequacy in consumers, selling advertising to those whose products offer to alleviate that sense of inadequacy. Whether the product is alcohol, cars, cigarettes, underwear, or appliances, the promise is the same: Use this and your anxiety will subside. Sociologist C. Wright Mills observed this dynamic in 1959, and it's truer today than ever before.

Three prevalent misunderstandings about fantasies and feelings contribute to our desire for secrecy. The first is that we are responsible for our fantasies and feelings; that if we are strong-willed, emotionally healthy, or highly spiritual, we will not create unusual or troubling mental images.

This simply is not true. As educator Sol Gordon says in his book, *The New You:* "Sexual thoughts, dreams, and daydreams are normal, no matter how far out. Behavior can be wrong, but ideas cannot be. Guilt provides the energy for the repetition of unacceptable thoughts. The best way of keeping unacceptable thoughts under control is to accept them as normal."

Dr. Gordon gives an excellent example: A fifteen-year-old boy accidentally glimpses his sister showering. Momentarily excited, he feels evil and guilty for enjoying it. In reaction, he becomes hostile to his sister. As her naked image refuses to leave his mind, he becomes increasingly depressed. Had he understood that his excitement was normal, he could have allowed the image to fade by itself, along with the incident's importance. Or he could have simply enjoyed it.

According to the "you are responsible" concept, fantasies reflect the gap between who we are and who we should be. What an unfair, unnatural standard to hold ourselves to. The belief that our fantasies indicate what we want, what we think we deserve, or what we feel is right is a grave moral error. It undermines the grand experience of taking responsibility for what we *can* control—our behavior.

The second frequent misunderstanding about fantasies and feelings is that they should be taken at face value.

Now sometimes fantasies are definitely about what they seem to be about. When we conjure up images of an exotic stranger while masturbating, for example, pure sexual pleasure is generally just what we have in mind. Why do we deliberately fantasize? Because it's enjoyable, of course.

There is, however, another side to consider about fantasies and feelings.

You've certainly had the experience of snapping at family or friends when you're really upset about your job. And you've probably barked at a colleague once or twice because you were aggravated about heavy traffic on the way to the office. These are ways of expressing feelings indirectly; that is, expressing one feeling rather than another one that lies underneath.

It's the same with fantasies. Instead of focusing on their content, we may understand them better by examining their theme or tone. For in the unconscious (as reflected, say, in dreams and verbal slips), "Logic carries no weight," said Freud, "contradictory urges or ideas exist side by side." Adult considerations such as the literal truth are irrelevant to the unconscious. Its goal is merely to express emotional energy.

Look at the following examples of "troubling" sexual fantasies. Acting out these images would certainly cause problems and invite judgment. As fantasies, however, their themes express understandable and "normal" feelings that we all share. See if you agree with the suggested interpretations.

⋄ *Fantasy:* A fifty-year-old man daydreams about making love with teenage girls walking past his car as he waits at a red light.
  Possibly expressing: The desire to be carefree and/or youthful again.
⋄ *Fantasy:* A heterosexual college student imagines a homosexual orgy with his basketball teammates.

Possibly expressing: The desire to feel part of a special group, like a family.

⬦ *Fantasy:* A woman heightens the excitement and pleasure of love-making by imagining she's being raped.

Possibly expressing: After a week of feeling powerless at work and at home, she seizes control by mentally directing intense, aggressive power.

⬦ *Fantasy:* A devoted grandmother of three fantasizes about seducing each of the four workmen on her roof.

Possibly expressing: Concerns about still being and feeling sexy and attractive.

⬦ *Fantasy:* A powerful executive masturbates to images of a man being tied up by a mean-looking woman dressed entirely in leather.

Possibly expressing: The wish to relinquish control or unload an overwhelming responsibility.

⬦ *Fantasy:* A woman compulsively reads romance novels and imagines herself as the heroine who is forced to submit to sex with a cruel stranger.

Possibly expressing: The wish to be valued so much that a man dishonors himself in order to pursue her.

Most fantasies reflect either unconscious processes or the desire to satisfy basic emotional needs. This is why we can neither rationally evaluate them nor trust their literal content. And it is why they provide such valuable emotional release, and why they must *not* be subject to the same standards as behavior.

Make no mistake, however: You and I are typically unaware of such themes when we create our fantasies. Our only awareness in generating these images is that they enrich our sexual satisfaction.

A third misunderstanding concerns the shamefulness of allegedly "bad" thoughts. People often express their fear of such thoughts by describing a sense of vulnerability and powerlessness. These feelings can be a dreadful reminder of adolescence, when new, unwanted sexual thoughts begin to appear without warning.

Here's how Phyllis, a pharmacist, wife, and mother, describes her current experience: "Sometimes I feel like someone's taken over my head. I see a man in the market and I imagine going right over and asking to play with his cock.

"Of course I don't do it," she quickly adds, "but it disturbs me that the image comes to mind. It makes me feel that I've got to watch myself every second."

Many women enjoy creating such fantasies. "It makes marketing much less of a chore," says Phyllis. Still, many worry that the fantasizing isn't normal, and they wonder if they should stop.

"I'll be in bed with my husband," Phyllis continues, "and right in the middle of sex I'll think, 'What if I don't come tonight? What if I never do again? It would just about ruin everything.' Fears like that—totally unrealistic, out of the blue—plus those supermarket feelings, make me worry that it's a mistake to just be myself. And all the while I'm smiling at my Harold, pretending that I'm calm, that there's no inner struggle."

Modern notions of morality focus far more on sexuality than on other aspects of daily life. As a result, institutions of authority claim the right to decide which expressions of sexuality are "normal." Typically we judge the discrepancies between ourselves and these norms as a problem with us, rather than with the norms. Predictably, this response is reinforced by the dominant culture. This dynamic is also discussed as a form of social pressure later in this chapter.

Why do we hide
our fantasies and feelings?

Various forms of the Secrecy Imperative explain much of the common drive toward keeping sexual fantasies and feelings secret. A look at child-hood—specifically the structure of a child's thought processes—will help us understand the feelings that typically surround adult fantasy life.

In 1921, Swiss psychologist Jean Piaget began to document the ways children think differently than adults. Concluding that the brain's men-tal capacities develop in an orderly, predictable fashion, he categorized the kinds of thinking characteristic at each stage of childhood.

Piaget observed that children actively create and recreate their models of reality as they understand the world in increasingly complex terms. Paradoxically, part of that complexity includes understanding the true separateness and limited power of individual human beings.

Most relevant for our discussion are these points of Piaget's:

- ♦ A preschooler's notion of causality is "magical." She believes that objects or events can act on each other simply because they are close to each other. For example, if you note how a box of fudge fits nicely on a shelf next to the milk, she might easily respond, "The milk moved over to make enough room for the fudge."

- ♦ A six-year-old cannot generally differentiate between the mental and the physical. His notion of causality is still magical, but now includes his own thoughts as an important agent of cause. If, while in the throes of a tantrum, he says he doesn't care if his frog dies, and the frog dies soon after, he could easily believe that he caused the frog's death.

- ♦ Preadolescents understand that their thoughts can't make objects move, but they still believe that their thoughts can be read by others or can influence them. An eleven-year-old may worry that she is the only one in her class who hasn't started menstruating. When another girl looks at her in the locker room, the eleven-year-old might believe the other girl knows what she's thinking.

✧ Adolescents understand the limits of their thoughts, but they judge and then overgeneralize the moral meaning of those thoughts. For example, a white teen doesn't like another teen who happens to be black, from the very first impression. On reflection, the white boy might think, "That is prejudice, which is bad. I must be completely prejudiced, therefore I am completely bad."

✧ Children can develop a moral system only as quickly as their thinking apparatus develops. A three-year-old can't really consider another's feelings because she cannot yet fully conceptualize the idea of "other." On the other hand, junior high school students express heightened interest in justice and fair play because they've started to develop the ability to think abstractly.

Thus, children learn to identify with and then separate from their thoughts in stages. "Realistic" and "logical" thought can only come in adulthood. And yet, all children strive mightily to make sense of the world around them. Doing so with the limited mental tools of childhood leads to some distorted, sadly destructive, results—like the Secrecy Imperative.

If one word sums up the world of the child, it is "magical." Not the magic of rabbits pulled from hats, but of various sources of power. One is the power of mere thought. Do you recall learning the following magic as a child?

◇ God knows all your thoughts (especially the bad ones).

◇ People can tell what you're thinking.

◇ Bad thoughts lead to nightmares.

◇ Bad thoughts can hurt people.

◇ Bad thoughts cause pimples, deformities, and accidents.

◇ Only bad people think bad thoughts.

◇ Thinking about doing something bad is as wrong as doing it.

As this list reveals, "bad thoughts" are considered dangerous. Youngsters, delightedly experimenting with their wonderful new abilities, cannot understand that the power of their thoughts is limited.

In addition, children **judge** their thoughts and feelings, using highly simplistic moral criteria. Young children can only grasp "good" and "bad." They literally cannot understand subtle moral distinctions, such as extenuating circumstances, competing interests, saving face, or sacrificing a small principle to secure a larger one.

Unfortunately, the distorted beliefs about their thoughts blur the difference between private mental activity and public behavior. This inhibits their sense of owning their own minds, and makes imagination and creativity dangerous.

Since their ability to categorize is very primitive, children have trouble understanding what it is about a particular thought that makes it bad. The only plausible answer, for the child, is "everything," which includes the thinker as well.

It is only a short step, therefore, from "My thoughts are bad" to "I am bad." For example, almost all children wish to get rid of their infant siblings. But since they've been told this **wish** is bad, they feel guilty for **being** bad unless their parents make it clear that such feelings are normal.

The problems of self-esteem, fear of intimacy, and lack of self-control resulting from children criticizing their own thoughts are well documented. Many parents unwittingly encourage this distorted emotional development. Without thinking, they discount their child's feelings: "Oh, you don't hate your sister, nice girls don't hate anybody." Or, "You don't wish your uncle were dead. God punishes little boys who wish such things."

Understandably, children are slow to give up the imagined power that comes with believing in the magic of their thoughts. Parents who suggest that the thinker of the criticized behavior deserves criticism only help maintain this childhood illusion. And since all children have predictable, uninvited thoughts (like incest and murder wishes), many become highly self-critical. The childhood conclusion that "I am bad" can be devastating.

The adult need for secrecy about thoughts and fantasies is an obvious consequence of childhood lessons about bad thoughts and the badness of those who think them.

During adolescence, children of each gender learn new reasons why sexual anxiety is inappropriate (and, therefore to be kept secret). Boys learn that "real men" are sex experts, which makes any lack of confidence a betrayal of masculinity. Expecting this expertise, many women are turned off by any doubt or anxiety a man has about his adequacy.

Young women are, in fact, instructed to assume that men are sex experts. But they also learn that men's egos are fragile. Thus, if a woman is anxious about sex, it is an insult to her partner. The only other explanation is that she is not a "real woman"—that is, one who can relax and enjoy sex with a (presumed) "real man." So young men and women both learn that anxiety about sex is abnormal, a problem to be hidden, even though this is the standard experience. And so another seed of secrecy is sown.

Children learn to hide their anxiety about sexuality when they watch their parents criticize each other's sex-role performance. The message is clear: They learn it is dangerous to share fears around inadequacy.

An engineer named Ravi told me a poignant story about this. "When I was about ten," he said, "my dad was laid off. At first it was neat having him home all the time, but after a few months, the mood around the house became pretty grim. One night I awoke to my parents discussing it. My dad, he said he was scared that he'd never find work again, and my mother blew up.

"'I can handle you losing your job,' I remember her saying angrily. 'But you're scared, nervous about finding another one! What kind of man are you?' she yelled. 'What kind of man gets scared?' My father just burst into tears, and my mother left the room.

"That rejection has stayed crystal clear in my mind. I learned right then that hiding and protecting yourself was a damn smart thing to do." Ravi's mother must have been so frightened that she couldn't tolerate anyone around her being anxious—especially the person who was supposed to be taking care of her.

When children hear one adult tell another, "I'm upset," if the reply is, "Don't feel that way," the message that feelings are wrong is reinforced. Can't you just hear Cary Grant's response to all those distraught women, in film after film? "Now, now, stop crying. Don't be silly. There's nothing to be upset about." In real life, responses like that teach people to hide their feelings.

Cultural messages, social pressure

In addition to these dynamics, several kinds of social pressures encourage us to withhold our sexual feelings, anxieties, and fantasies.

The media present a remarkably homogeneous set of images. Advertisements, magazine covers, and TV and film stars all offer the same predictable portrait of attractiveness in men and women. In this way, we are instructed on the kind of fantasy object that is most acceptable. In fact, the media create and present the objects themselves, revering them as objects rather than as people. Our lust for them is impersonal precisely *because* they are public figures, completely unknown to us, and shared with millions of other adoring fans.

Our mates, to a degree, participate in our fantasies about celebrities. Your partner knows about the fantasy object, generally agrees that the object represents perfection, and even that the object is more attractive than he or she is. Few men need to hide the fact that they find Miss America hot. What we tend to hide is our attraction to a neighbor or colleague.

The media also encourage secrecy by invariably portraying heroes without sexual anxiety or other inconvenient feelings. Generations of men have modeled themselves after James Bond and John Wayne, icons who lack the normal anxiety, anger, disappointment, and frustration that interfere with the romantic relationships of real people.

Why aren't our relationships as perfect and thrilling as theirs? One reason is that James Bond isn't involved in intimacy. He's an object interacting with other objects. But real adults generally want this perfection *and* they want intimacy, which simply cannot be attained. In reaction, most of us deal with this discrepancy by hiding it. We develop the common belief that discussing anxiety or other feelings "breaks the mood" and creates distance.

Another social pressure encouraging secrecy is the cultural belief that certain thoughts are bad, and that thinking these thoughts is as bad as acting them out. We have already discussed how there are no bad thoughts, only bad—i.e., destructive—behaviors. But some religious traditions, unfortunately, make "bad thoughts" an absolute cornerstone of belief. According to the *New Catholic Encyclopedia*, "The act of thinking can be good or evil . . . . The attention of Catholic moralists has centered chiefly upon evil rather than upon good thoughts. Morality is primarily a matter of the heart; [this is recalled in the] Pauline theme of . . . the primacy of attitude over acts."

This view truly stands human experience on its head. Aren't most of us concerned first with how someone treats us, and only secondarily with what thoughts they have? Yet, this religious doctrine presumes to judge private thoughts, even to the exclusion of our righteous deeds.

And it goes even further. Look at how serious a moral crime it is to enjoy or even tolerate "sinful" fantasies or feelings: "The quality of the sin is the same as that of the corresponding exterior act; for example, an actual murder." In simple language: If doing something is evil, thinking about doing it without immediate moral judgment is *just as evil*.

No one who believes this doctrine would dare admit to a friend or loved one that he had done the spiritual equivalent of rape, incest, infidelity, group sex, or exposing himself. Realistically, people conceal such thoughts, condemning themselves as "perverse" or "kinky."

How do we maintain secrecy?

The secrets we have about our fantasies or anxieties are often hidden from ourselves as well as from others. We don't do this deliberately. Rather, we do it through unconscious maneuvers designed to keep us unaware of painful feelings. Freud called these maneuvers "defense mechanisms," mental activities meant to "defend" us from the pain of feeling guilty or evil for having unacceptable thoughts.

Let's look at how this is done.

The first defense is called **projection**. This is when you unconsciously attribute a feeling that you can't accept as your own to another person. People who project a lot get involved in needless conflict, as they respond to insults, threats, challenges, seductions, and other emotional events that aren't really there, or aren't about them.

One of the predictable results of projection is emotional distance. This was the problem for a forty-year-old man I counseled.

Julio was a county employee who married his college sweetheart, Lupe, the day after they graduated. Lupe insisted he see me because of his jealous rages. "He swears I'm having affairs," she said in exasperation, "which is crazy. He has no evidence, and I have no interest in other men. He says he knows that I love him. What's wrong with the guy?"

Julio turned out to be a warm, articulate man who was also confused by the situation. While acknowledging that he didn't have any real evidence of Lupe's cheating, he said that strong feelings periodically came over him without warning. At those times he would become nasty and difficult to live with.

How did a rational, intelligent man handle these irrational episodes? "I suppose you'd say that it's crazy to accuse her of cheating that way," he said blandly, "but maybe it isn't. After all, almost everyone has affairs, you know. Everyone but me."

It was an odd thing to say, so I asked Julio why he didn't have affairs. "I'm not that type," he said. "You know—selfish, irresponsible. Like my dad." He dropped the clue rather casually. Julio's father, apparently, had been the talk of their small Oregon town, sleeping with widows, teenagers, and hitchhikers with equal abandon. It had destroyed their family. "Worst of all," Julio later recalled bitterly, "the other kids teased me about it."

No wonder Julio was eager to dissociate himself from his destructive father. Unconsciously fearing his vulnerability to Lupe's behavior, he tried to control it with preemptive strikes. His accusations were, unconsciously, meant to prevent her from ruining his life, or to catch her trying to.

But I believed there was more. Did Julio ever daydream about having an affair of his own? "I told you," he said impatiently, "I've never had an affair. I never would." Could Julio differentiate between fantasy and behavior? I questioned him about daydreams once more, and received the same curt answer.

Taking a calculated risk, I pressed on. "Julio, many men think about having affairs, even if they never have them. Are you—"

"That's being unfaithful," he interrupted. "I wouldn't do that."

We were getting closer; I pushed again. "So when you see a beautiful woman in the street, or in a movie, do you—"

"I put it out of my mind!" he yelled. "I'm not going to let it control me. I won't let anyone know I think these things." He was shaking.

The room echoed with Julio's powerful emotions. Although his thoughts were quite common, he found them unacceptable. It was understandable, given his background. His dad's affairs had hurt the entire family, and Julio was determined that he wasn't going to do the same.

So what could he do with his "destructive" sexual thoughts about other people? Project them onto Lupe, and attempt to control them from a safer distance. Ironically, his unpredictable attacks created exactly the same isolation and sadness that he was trying so desperately to avoid. Julio had a secret: He thought about sex with other women. If he could only accept the normalcy of these thoughts, he would have many more options for dealing with them.

The following are other defense mechanisms we use to keep secrets from ourselves.

Repression is one way of hiding the truth from ourselves. Alcohol, tobacco, and other mind-altering chemicals are this culture's accepted medium for avoiding painful facts and feelings. They are also frequently used to create and maintain sexual secrets. Some men may never know they feel threatened by powerful women because they only go out (or make love) after they've had a joint or a few drinks.

Blame is another form of self-deception. We use blame when it's difficult to admit what we want, or when we feel more comfortable believing that others control our choices. Teenagers and others who have trouble taking responsibility for themselves often use this defense.

One woman I used to work with would become extremely aroused fantasizing about her husband with other women (which is fairly common). She said she wanted to share the fantasy in their lovemaking, but felt that she couldn't because he'd never stop talking about it. So she blamed her husband for preventing her from doing what she wanted, but couldn't bring herself to do.

Reaction formation involves doing the opposite of what you'd unconsciously like to do, but feel you must not. Some people want to ban nude beaches, for example, to prove to themselves that they don't really want to look at naked people—which they do. In this way they keep their secret from themselves, if not from cynical observers. The rest of us pay for their blissful self-ignorance with restrictions on our civil liberties.

Deception may be used to hide secrets about sex-related fear or anxiety. An oncology nurse named Ming Na came to see me about her difficulty climaxing. What made it a particular problem, she said, was her increased sex drive since her recent hysterectomy.

Ming Na was a bit older than many of the men in her department, and she felt she had to compete with younger women. She believed that they all had an easy time climaxing (not true), which would make her anxiety laughable to a new partner. On top of everything else, Ming Na also believed her anxiety would offend a lover, who would feel it reflected a lack of trust in his lovemaking ability.

To handle her anxiety, Ming Na hid it, and used marijuana before making love to help her relax and focus on the pleasure. Unfortunately, the grass was giving her a hangover, was sometimes difficult to hide, and was unhealthy. Although Ming Na was not addicted, she hesitated to stop because she had no other way of handling her anxiety.

Committed to secrecy about her feelings, Ming Na was really stuck. Above all, she needed to accept her anxiety as "normal," which would give her the choice of sharing it or concealing it. Either way, she would feel better about herself.

Denial is a familiar childhood method for attempting to keep a secret. It reflects the magical belief that if I say it isn't so, it isn't so. Denial is a very primitive, or childish, defense.

You've probably had the experience, during sex, of sensing that your partner was worried, nervous, or distracted. "What's the matter?" you gently inquire. "Nothing," you're told, or "Just a lot on my mind. Forget it."

This is the way we teach our partners to discount their senses and to go ahead with sex under negative conditions. The anxious partner also learns, one more time, that feeling isolated is the normal context of sexuality.

Then there's the other kind of denial, aimed toward limiting a partner's knowledge rather than our own. Satirist Lenny Bruce used to tell a story about the way some men denied their sexual feelings or behavior despite the most blatant evidence to the contrary.

"A woman suspects her husband's infidelity for a long time, but has no proof. One day she comes home early and finds him in bed with another woman. 'It's not what you think,' he says to her calmly. 'You miserable clog,' she shouts. 'Now, dear, it's not what it looks like,' he suggests genially. 'You can't be trusted one bit,' she cries. 'Honey,' the man soothes, 'who are you going to believe—your loving husband or your lying eyes?' "

Fantasies

According to Masters and Johnson, "Sexual fantasies begin in childhood and serve us in important ways, such as combating boredom, providing or enhancing excitement, releasing inner tensions, and permitting safe, imaginary rehearsals of untried behavior." They continue into adulthood, serving these and other purposes.

As sexologist Dr. Charles Moser says, "No one can imagine the entire range of typical sexual fantasies, no matter how outrageous his own fantasies are." And yet, secrecy prevents people from knowing how common their own fantasies are.

Secrecy about fantasies has the same isolating, demeaning effects as other sexual secrets. Of course, not every fantasy is best revealed—lust for your brother-in-law may be better kept from your sister—but, as we've seen all along, more important than the revelation of your secrets is the acceptance that they are normal. Two related stories make this point.

When John called me to set up our first appointment, he said he was worried about his mental health. On the day of our first session, a virtual twin of Alan Alda walked in. He had a warm and gentle manner. After some pleasant preliminaries, he told me about his loneliness.

"It's simple," he said, "when I masturbate I think of doing things that worry me. Like I'm forcing women to have oral sex with me, or I'm seducing young girls. I even imagine getting my brother's wife drunk and half raping her," he said ruefully.

"I'd never do these things. So why do I think about them? Why do they make my orgasms so fabulous? I feel very alone," John continued. "Who can I tell about this? Nobody. Nobody I ever want to see again, that's for sure."

Poor John. He didn't understand that such fantasies are very common. And, of course, the overwhelming majority of people with such fantasies have no interest in acting them out. I told John I accepted him regardless of his fantasies. It was a powerful experience for him, being fully accepted after revealing his darkest secrets. I don't think he ever told anyone else about his fantasies, but he did begin to accept himself. That was what he needed the most.

Here's another view of the same story; call it the other side of the coin, if you wish.

A well-known author I'll call Cindy came to see me. "Sex is fine, better than fine," she started, "except for one thing. I have this totally unacceptable fantasy. It's big black men holding me down, taking turns screwing me. In the fantasy I have one giant orgasm after another, which triggers the real thing."

And that was totally unacceptable? "Yes," she answered emphatically. "It's just not me, that powerless crap. You know where I am politically." Indeed, I was very familiar with her views. "I feel guilty and very embarrassed about these fantasies," she continued. "But I love them. They make my orgasms incredibly hot, whether I'm alone or with a man."

Cindy felt she couldn't share her distress, not with her lovers and certainly not with her feminist friends. Her embarrassment was additional proof, she reasoned, that the fantasies were bad. "Or maybe I'm not the committed feminist I thought I was," she said. "That would kill me."

Neither Cindy nor John understood the nature of fantasy, nor the concept that **thinking** about a situation does not mean **desiring** it. Why then did they fantasize behavior that they had no interest in carrying out?

As therapist Jack Morin, author of *The Erotic Mind*, says, "Almost everyone fantasizes. And in order to intensify our sexual response, we produce fantasies in which we overcome some psychological distance. That distance can involve, for example, taboos or physical danger, both very common fantasy themes." That certainly describes both Cindy's and John's fantasies. Both scenarios allow responses to situations that are not "supposed" to be enjoyed. This element alone creates tremendous arousal.

The troubling fantasies that people hide range from the exotic to the homespun. After a lecture I gave in Pittsburgh, a woman approached me. "I love my husband, Dimitri, very much," she said. "But sometimes I think about Denzel Washington when I make love with him. It troubles me." She seemed to need reassurance very much.

"Don't you think Dimitri would agree," I asked, "that fantasizing about Denzel Washington while making love with your husband is preferable to thinking of your husband while making love to Denzel Washington?"

She thought about it and began to smile. "I guess it's like you said in your talk," she mused. "If it works for me, it defines what's normal for me, right?"

I smiled as broadly as she did. "Right," I said, with great satisfaction.

Anxiety: a pathway to intimacy?

Human beings experience a remarkable range of feelings, and anxiety is one of the most prevalent and unpleasant. Mental health professionals unanimously agree that anxiety plays a destructive role in sexual functioning.

Bernie Zilbergeld wrote in *Male Sexuality* that sexual messages from the brain to the genitals "must be clearly sent and received. If the nervous system is obstructed, the messages to the [genitals] don't get through properly. The most common obstructor during sex is nervous tension or anxiety. [It] throws the whole nervous system into a tizzy, obstructing the transmission of sexual messages."

What's worse than feeling anxious? The certainty that you must keep quiet about the anxiety. The following story illustrates this point.

Naomi was sent to me by her company's personnel counselor because of complaints that she wasn't self-directed enough. I quickly saw that she wanted to please everyone, and felt incapable of doing so.

As our work together progressed, Naomi realized that she wanted more supervision on the job, along with more support and encouragement. Eventually she was able to ask for these changes, and her performance improved almost immediately. At that point she asked if we could talk about her marriage, especially about sex.

"I worry a lot," she said simply. "Am I really satisfying my husband? Does he like my body? What if he's holding back because of me? How do you know if you're good in bed?" She didn't dare tell her husband, but Naomi had a sexual secret: She was anxious about her adequacy.

It was similar to her work issue. She needed to feel more connected to those around her. But she wasn't sure she deserved it, and wasn't comfortable asking for it.

Where had she gotten the idea that she wasn't sexually adequate? "Well," she started, "I was taught that you're either a nice girl or a sexy bad one, right? Of course, I like to think I'm one of the nice girls. Besides, the sexy ones are young and slim. These thighs will never see twenty-five again," she chuckled sadly.

As I listened, I noted Naomi's assumptions that she had to choose between being nice *or* being sexy, that "of course" she'd choose the former, and that there was only one way to define sexy. Rather than abruptly confront her about these notions, I encouraged her to continue. I knew we'd return to these ideas eventually.

Continuing, Naomi revealed that a series of emotionally abusive "normal" boyfriends were also part of the picture. "My college boyfriend? He called himself 'a man's man' and said I was lucky that he was my first. Afterward he told me I was lucky that he had been so patient. He made it clear that I wasn't, and would never be, really sexy."

Nice guy, I thought to myself. *He* should pay for the therapy. Because, now that Naomi is married, she's unsure of her sexual attractiveness. Worse still, she can't share her concerns with her husband. "He'd take it personally," she said, believing that this was a good enough reason to isolate herself. "It's better that he doesn't know what's wrong."

In reality, Naomi's silence reflects **her** judgment about her insecurity, not her husband's. She simply believes it's wrong to feel that way, and that no man should be asked to deal with it. Naomi is hypersensitive to anything that looks like a demand, fearing she'll be abandoned if she asks for anything.

Secrecy about performance anxiety takes many forms. Because of early lessons about "manliness," this tends to be a particularly problematic experience for men.

The subject reminds me of Lamar, a big, likable guy who was a brakeman on a San Francisco cable car. He enjoyed his work, especially the chance to meet so many people. His friendliness made it easy to start relationships, both with tourists and locals.

"I'm here to talk about dating," he began our first session. "Everything goes fine, until it's clear that the woman is interested in sex. Then something happens. We get into a fight, I decide it wasn't such a good idea, one of us loses interest, whatever. I'm really mystified," he said. "And horny."

I wondered why a man who enjoyed making contact with people kept arranging not to have sex. While talking about what he liked and disliked about lovemaking, Lamar mentioned his concern about "doing it right." He said he wanted to be "the best lover in the world," but he sometimes worried that he wasn't.

Did he share this anxiety with his lovers? "No," he said, "of course not." And why not? He looked at me, somewhat confused. "No one does, do they? I mean, I wouldn't think of telling a woman I was concerned about my performance."

When I again asked Lamar why not, he said he didn't have a specific reason. "It's something I've always taken for granted." Then I ran down a list of some common feelings that people feel they shouldn't talk about, feelings that may oblige us to hide our anxiety about sex. Was it any of these?

- ⬧ You'll think I'm silly.
- ⬧ I don't know how you'll respond.
- ⬧ I don't feel close enough to you for such intimate sharing.
- ⬧ It will make my anxiety worse.
- ⬧ You'll leave me.

No, it wasn't any of these, Lamar said, growing more restless by the minute. "I've had enough questions," he boomed. "I hate feeling this way. It's totally uncool to worry about your damn hard-on . . . the hell with sex!" The room was silent.

I observed the outburst calmly, without replying. Clearly, Lamar had sexual anxiety, and, just as clearly, he was ashamed of it. Therefore he tried to hide it. And the way he hid it was by unconsciously aborting potential sexual interactions. That allowed him to avoid the painful possibility of not performing perfectly.

"You know," I finally said, "you're not the first person to raise his voice in this room." Lamar looked at me quizzically. "In fact, everyone with your sexual concern gets upset one way or another. I guess I'm more used to it than you are." Lamar wasn't sure how to take this, so I continued.

"People don't need good reasons to be concerned about their sexual performance," I said. "Look around you. Television, movies, and magazines can scare someone enough to swear off sex altogether. And," I added, "make you think you're the only one who feels that way."

As Lamar slowly smiled, I knew I'd gotten through to him. "You're saying it is normal to be nervous," he said. "I bet you're even going to say that it's normal to try and hide it." I simply nodded, letting him enjoy the insight.

A second type of anxiety involves privacy, specifically the concern that a partner will reveal the relationship to others. Privacy is typically an issue when a relationship involves social or economic concerns to the outside world. Examples include:

⋄ A man is having an affair with a woman who doesn't know that he's married.

⋄ An executive is seeing someone on her company's maintenance staff.

⋄ A woman has a well-cultivated reputation as a virgin.

⋄ A middle-aged professor is dating a college student.

⋄ A shy woman does not want to be known as someone with a very high sex drive.

⋄ A man knows his partner is sexually dissatisfied.

The Secrecy Imperative explains why we typically choose not to share privacy anxieties. We believe we shouldn't have such feelings, and assume that our partners would judge them, and us, if they knew the truth.

In some cases, these concerns are based on reality. The maintenance worker, for example, might feel angry that his management girlfriend does not want anyone to know they are lovers. Some partners even end relationships once they discover why privacy is desired. This often happens with extramarital affairs in which an unmarried lover has been deceived.

But in many cases our partners understand our need for privacy. Even when they don't, they often choose to respect it anyway. There are many other reasons for keeping their anxiety secret:

⋄ I'm not supposed to care about keeping our relationship private.

⋄ I don't want to acknowledge that you have power over me.

⋄ I feel embarrassed about being anxious.

⋄ I don't want to appear foolish.

⋄ I'm afraid you'll feel that I don't trust you.

Such concepts can be traced back to the Secrecy Imperative. They are nearly always projections of our own feelings and self-criticism onto those close to us.

The woman with the virginal reputation, for example, knows she is deceiving people. She feels guilty about it, and projects her guilt onto her lover, believing **he** couldn't handle her anxiety about losing her valued reputation.

There's an irony about "anxiety secrecy" worth noting here. Many people believe that talking about anxiety makes it worse. Keeping your anxiety secret from your lover removes the most effective anti-anxiety tool, which is talking about the feelings. There may be costs to doing so—there is the risk of rejection—but that does not negate the point. Talking about anxiety almost invariably **reduces** it. In fact, talking about anxiety is a great way to get close to someone. Secrecy makes that conversation impossible.

Talking about anxiety makes intimacy possible. Some people feel that this is worth just about any risk.

Fear, anger, and other feelings

Fear and anger are two other feelings often associated with sex. Many men and women feel obligated to keep these secret because of social pressure. "You're not supposed to have those feelings about sex," states one client angrily. "And if you do, they are not supposed to affect your behavior."

Bernie Zilbergeld wrote in *Male Sexuality*, "There is a common belief that the second we get involved in a sexual situation, we should be able to put our feelings aside. I have worked with many men, for example, who demand that they be able to get erections even with women they don't like. To me, that's one way to create sexual problems."

Many of us need educating about this exact point. One of the nicer people I have worked with was Janelle, whose complaint was lack of orgasm. A medical review showed no physiological problem. "I don't expect to climax every time I make love," she said, "but I would like to come much more often."

A few weeks later, Janelle came to our session with her boyfriend, Mark, a professional baseball player. They don't look that big on TV, but this guy just about filled up the waiting room.

I don't recall exactly how it came up, but we were soon talking about "perfect" sex. "It would be better for me," said Janelle quietly, "if you were smaller." Mark was genuinely surprised. "I thought you loved my body!" "I do," Janelle continued, "but it's also, umm, overwhelming. You don't know how scary you can be." Surprised herself to hear the words, she looked away.

Hurt, Mark lashed out. "I don't understand. I try to be a good lover, don't I? I'm always gentle. What are you afraid of? Why are you so hung up on me saying I love you?"

"Because sex is scary, period," Janelle replied. "If *you* were on your back naked, and someone twice your size was bouncing around on top of you *and* had part of their body inside yours, you might be nervous too," she said. "I bet you'd want to hear 'I love you' a lot."

The secret was out: Janelle wanted more **attention** during sex. All three of us now understood her lack of orgasms, which wasn't so odd after all.

I suggested that she and Mark discuss specific ways they could make sex more **personal.** "Hey, I wouldn't mind some more of that myself," Mark said with a laugh. They agreed to work on it together at home.

Another woman who had difficulty climaxing was Tracy, a newlywed. "I don't understand it," she said at our first session. "The sex is great. Josh is a fabulous lover. So why is it getting harder and harder for me to come?"

I asked about her new marriage. It was terrific, Tracy exclaimed. She loved "our house, our dog, his parents, our parties, my new job ...."

Notice what's missing? What about their relationship? That, it turned out, wasn't quite perfect. "I guess we argue a lot," admitted Tracy. "And you know men. When Josh doesn't get his way, he loses his temper. Sometimes he leaves the house."

Every marriage, of course, has conflict, but partners need to know they can express themselves without being punished. Tracy knew just the opposite: Telling the truth about her needs and feelings would result in being attacked or abandoned. And so, very often, she didn't.

How did she feel about that? "Oh, okay. Maybe a little irritated," she said. I looked at her and said nothing. "Okay, more than a little," she offered. "Okay, I'm angry, so what? That doesn't solve anything, does it?" Tears started to form in her eyes. "Besides, that shouldn't stop me from coming."

Josh didn't really know the extent of her anger, did he? "No," Tracy sniffed. "He'd yell or call me names. Probably leave for the day. I'm better off this way," she said.

"Not as far as sex goes," I said gently. Her body was saying what the rest of her couldn't: "I'm angry. I feel abandoned. It isn't safe to be me here."

Orgasms require letting go. Tracy couldn't come easily because the marriage had no room for her to let go and be herself. The fact that she couldn't discuss her feelings with Josh illustrated that perfectly.

Tracy left my office unsure of what she'd do. She wanted to keep her feelings to herself a while longer, hoping a new position or a weekend away would improve their sex life. I doubted it. When the brain and genitals disagree, the genitals always win. Tracy's vulva would keep expressing the outrage that the rest of her felt.

Tracy and Josh finally reached the point where they were willing to try **anything** to make sex better. Therapy was painful at times, but it was successful. Not only did sex become more rewarding, they learned how to talk to each other about many other things as well.

◎◎

Feelings and thoughts are the building blocks of human relationships. Judging them to be "incorrect," or hiding them, strikes at the heart of our dignity and self-esteem. How do people feel when they hide sexual thoughts and feelings? Lonely, isolated, angry, inadequate, phony, afraid of discovery, and prone to anxiety.

We are a society with rigid cultural standards about "proper" feelings and thoughts. These standards make secrecy about feelings and fantasies seem necessary—which makes them destructive.

Freeing ourselves from the compulsive need to be proper is an important part of growing up. At the same time, establishing reasonable limits for ourselves is also important. Finding a healthy balance between the two is one of the great challenges of adulthood.

Chapter 6

Sexual Secrets:
The Past

◎◎

Why allow the ghosts of the past to determine what you can do today?

—SOL GORDON

As you know, the focus of this book is not simply **revealing** your sexuality, but **owning** it. I would like to help you decide that regardless of your judgements (or those of others, real or imagined), you are okay. Some people call this forgiving yourself. Others say it involves reclaiming your past.

What would you be forgiving? Past choices and experiences that you might arrange differently if given the chance today. Or past choices and experiences that you feel fine about, but your lover has a problem with. A friend of mine, for example, did not tell her fiancé she was sterile until after they were engaged. She'd tell him sooner if she could do it all over again, but she recognizes today that at the time, she was doing the best she could.

And what would you be reclaiming? The reality that your past behavior is part of you. A great example, still relevant after thirty years, occurred in 1972. A group of women, organized by Gloria Steinem, signed a full-page ad in *The New York Times* affirming that each had had

103

an illegal abortion. The ad demanded that abortion be legalized.

The chance to make peace with yourself is the first important reason to discuss your secret-keeping about the past. As you'll see in this chapter, if you're willing to reclaim the past, you can:

⬧ Allow yourself to forgive others.
⬧ Redistribute power in your relationships.
⬧ Free your future from imagined constraints.

How does reclaiming the past do these things? First, it allows us to stop hiding. We can still regret something we've done, or accept it. Moving beyond it allows us to contact others with our full selves. As we have seen throughout this book, such contact is an important key to relationship and life satisfaction.

Second, reclaiming the past interrupts the common life script of "Because of what I did in the past, I don't get (nor do I deserve) good things." Such a script is responsible for chronic self-destructive patterns, such as remaining in relationships with alcoholics; failing to advance in our jobs, schools, or volunteer organizations; or an inability to permanently quit smoking cigarettes.

Owning your past lets you see yourself as a good person who made particular choices, one who still deserves good things regardless of the outcome of those choices. It also gives you the freedom to determine your own life, instead of feeling that it is predetermined by the past.

This "get on with it" attitude is the opposite of "I'll never escape the fact that I was born on the wrong side of the tracks," or "I was a bad girl back then and I'll be paying for it the rest of my life."

And owning your past, finally, lets you reintegrate lost parts of yourself. When we are children survival often seems to require giving up our intuition, openness, and willingness to experiment. But those qualities are part of us. Welcoming them back into your psyche is like welcoming home an old friend whom you didn't realize you missed so badly.

After you have accepted yourself, you can experience the true option of revealing sexual secrets about your past.

How do we feel about the past? How do you?

During a typical week, I meet many people with strong feelings about their sexual past. Most of them feel alone, doubting that anyone could understand their situation or be in a similar one. How do we feel about the past?

- ◇ "It feels like it happened to someone else."
- ◇ "I was foolish," or "I made mistakes."
- ◇ "If I'm not careful it will sneak up and get me."

Think about how you feel about your own past. Are you aware of any of these common feelings?

- ◇ I should have known better.
- ◇ I asked for trouble.
- ◇ I don't deserve good things.
- ◇ I judge my past behavior by my present wisdom and needs.
- ◇ I should be judged more harshly than others.
- ◇ I deserve punishment for being victimized.
- ◇ Certain things should not be forgiven.
- ◇ Forgiveness means approval.
- ◇ The past has no logic of its own.
- ◇ My past is worse than everyone else's.
- ◇ No one would understand how it was.

Can you see how such feelings would distort your evaluation of your past and the way others react to it? These feelings are intimately connected to the four principal reasons we keep our past secret:

1. We have an inaccurate view of the past.
2. We wish to pursue other goals.
3. Relationship dynamics don't permit honesty.
4. Cultural concepts encourage silence.

Let's examine each one in turn.

The Secrecy Imperative distorts our view of the past. This is particularly true regarding our assumptions:

⬦ The seriousness of what we've done is too awful to be shared.
⬦ The consequences of what we've done are too embarassing to be disclosed.
⬦ Others will react (negatively) to what we've done.
⬦ We should be judged (harshly) for what we've done.

Take Monica, a thirty-five-year-old accountant. She never had casual flings; in fact, when an irritating vaginal sore was diagnosed as herpes several years ago, she was in the middle of a period of abstinence. Monica was shocked and repulsed.

"I don't even know who I got it from," she cried. "How's that for prim and proper?" (The virus can lie dormant for years before the first outbreak.) "I feel dirty and guilty," she continued angrily. "That's why I don't tell anyone about it." She stays away from sex during an outbreak, which is about twice a year.

Unfortunately, Monica has had a string of unsatisfying relationships since her first outbreak. She doesn't believe that a "nice guy" would be interested in "damaged goods," and so she unconsciously avoids nice guys. As damaged goods, she doesn't feel she deserves any better than the dependent, selfish jerks who have been ripping her off for three years. She's paying for her "unacceptable" past, unnecessarily.

Given her frustration with the way things worked out, what should Monica have done differently? Should she have been celibate? More "careful"? (She *was* careful, but even "nice, clean" people get herpes.) In any event, Monica has made her decisions. Although she may regret some of them (hindsight, after all, is 20/20), she certainly doesn't deserve punishment.

Unfortunately, Monica cannot see that. Her judgment is clouded by a punitive Secrecy Imperative that distorts her view of her behavior's consequences. Her inner voice says, "If it's about me and my sexuality, it must be bad." Monica's punitive side uses the herpes as proof. Her self-criticism is particularly ironic when compared with the loving support she'd give a friend in the same circumstances.

Once again, the Secrecy Imperative distorts our perceptions about the way we manifest our sexuality. It makes us harsh critics—unfair prosecutors rather than fair magistrates.

So how can you establish a balanced perspective about your past?

⋄ Become aware of judging yourself. Instead of taking your internal critical voice for granted, recognize it as an unwanted mental intrusion. Whenever Monica thinks of herself as "damaged goods," she must remind herself, "No, I am not. I simply have a common virus which affects my life very little."

⋄ Become absolutely clear that you can be okay regardless of your past decisions. Monica at some point chose to have unprotected sex. As a person, Monica is far bigger than this or any other decision she has made. Having resumed using condoms, she has no reason to keep castigating herself.

- ◇ Create new, explicit, gentle criteria with which to appraise yourself. For example, "Am I learning from past outcomes?" "How am I dealing with the sources of distortion and negativity?"
- ◇ Reward yourself whenever you meet those criteria. Be open to evidence that you are growing as a self-loving person, and then celebrate it. Buy yourself a small treat. Take a friend to lunch. Pay to have your car washed.
- ◇ Become aware of people or situations by which you are predictably attacked, and take positive steps to cope with or eliminate those relationships. If a seven-day family visit always involves five days of criticism and domination, make it a three-day visit instead, or even two separate one-day visits.

A second reason to keep quiet about the past is that we use secrecy to pursue unconscious goals. For some, the past contains more excitement than shame. One of my Asian clients, for example, frequently reminisces about the black men she had sex with before marrying her husband. This kind of secrecy is often a form of nostalgia. It offers a way to keep alive a past in which we felt more attractive, or fuller of potential, or able to enjoy life with less responsibility.

Although we may convince ourselves that this secrecy is crucial, it may primarily express our commitment to hold on to the past. While grieving for our losses is difficult, the payoff is fuller commitment to the present.

Secrecy about the past also offers the chance to play out our destructive personality scripts. Take someone who grew up in an abusive home, like Natalie. Very early, Natalie developed the belief that men are no good and that trusting them is a mistake. As an adult, she unconsciously pursues this conviction in every relationship. She does this by hiding her past which makes closeness difficult. In addition to her abusive background, she withholds anything about herself that could facilitate intimacy. Another client hides the fact that she wrote erotic poetry in college. Another conceals the story of her two-year engagement to a marine killed in the Gulf War. All of these women can "prove" how hard it is to be close to men.

Playing out such a script also encourages a partner's secrecy. Natalie and people like her often feel insecure when given information about their partner's past. "I knew I shouldn't have trusted you," she said after a boyfriend revealed he had once been caught exposing himself in public. "You're probably dying to do it again," she said bitterly. Such a reaction often brings about the very behavior that is feared. Once more, Natalie would get to be right.

A third reason for secrecy is that certain relationship dynamics exploit the past. Some people use a partner's past to control the current relationship they're in. A college-graduate wife may continually remind her college-dropout husband: "You're good with your hands, dear, but leave the thinking to me." Another tactic is to comment on a mate's personal history in public. One jealous man, for example, loudly mentions his wife's background as a topless dancer whenever they're at a party where she gets any male attention.

These forms of manipulation make a partner feel powerless and vulnerable. Each of us has the right to decide what parts of our past are beyond routine comment via teasing, questions, or arguments.

If you can't seem to get a partner to respect your decisions about your past, assume that some kind of power play is going on and address it on that level: "Steve, I've said that your continual reminders of my affair during my first marriage are very uncomfortable for me, yet you persist. What could you be getting out of this that is more important to you than my discomfort?"

Steve's unwanted teasing makes his wife regret telling him of her affair. Secrecy is a natural impulse for people who have their past used against them.

The anticipation of criticism also discourages disclosure. When a loved one says, "We all know that group sex is bad," we typically translate that to mean, "Don't reveal that you've had group sex."

So, you can understand the importance of the question: Who gets to decide what parts of your past are eligible for criticism? Is it your decision, which your partner agrees to? Or do others (spouse, parent, or even child) impose their judgements on you? I believe it should be your decision alone, and I encourage you to reject others' attempts to impose their values on you.

Why? Because we resist values that others impose on us. At most, we tolerate them, but such tolerance is short-lived. Eventually, we grow resentful about not having the space we need to be ourselves. We might even deliberately violate the imposed values to assert our independence. As you know, teens do this all the time.

If a couple has seriously contrasting values, professional help may be needed in order for them to live harmoniously. Unresolved, serious values conflicts often breed mistrust, hostility, and secrecy.

When one person in a relationship imposes his or her sexual values on the other, two basic questions are raised:

1. Why is Partner One doing that to Partner Two?
2. Why is Partner Two allowing Partner One to do it?

Why is your lover doing this to you? When values are imposed on you, the past can be redefined. Being bullied into believing that you were corrupted in college by your gay friend, for example, and dropping your belief that you were consciously experimenting, changes the meaning of your previous relationships, choices, and identity.

When our partners redefine our past it is a means of controlling us.

Imposing values on you can be a selfish, unfair way for your partner to handle some of these common feelings:

◇ "I'm uncomfortable with your definition of your past."
◇ "I feel left out of your past. I don't want it to be complete or satisfactory without me."
◇ "I'm afraid I can't stop you from repeating that in the future."

A typical situation of controlling-by-imposing-values is a man who attempts to redefine the sexually active past of a new girlfriend. Although most men want their partners to be interested in sex with them, many are uncomfortable with the idea of free-floating female sexuality. Their feeling could be described as, "I want a woman's sexual interest to lie dormant, except when directed toward me personally."

This, of course, is not always the reality, particularly as more and more women seize their own power and independence. Still, some men will "explain" a woman's sexual history by suggesting that she was "going through a phase," "rebelling," "experimenting," or even that she was "exploited." All of which is to say that her behavior was unacceptable. Which leads her to keep it under wraps.

Back to question 2: Why do we allow our lovers to impose their sexual values on us?

We give away the power to define our sexual past for several reasons. For starters, the Secrecy Imperative pushes us in that direction. We think, "If it's my sexuality, it's suspect. If you say that someone like me is bad, you're probably right."

A slightly different version of this dynamic is: "You think someone like me is immoral. I'm not positive, but you may be right. And if I disagree with you, you'll feel certain that I'm immoral, and you may be even more right. So to play it safe, I'll let you decide what kind of past is appropriate, and I'll hide anything that doesn't fit that standard."

Believing the other person knows better is a common reason for relinquishing power. This is illustrated in the following two-part story. I'll present it in chronological order, although it wasn't given to me in such a convenient form.

Between her first and second marriages, a realtor named Janice went to Lake Tahoe for a long weekend with a girlfriend. They had a great time and became very close, and on their last night in the mountains they made love. "I had wondered what it would be like," said Janice, "and the moment, somehow, was perfect."

Even though they both enjoyed the experience, they had no interest in pursuing that part of their relationship. They are still friends. In fact, Pam was maid of honor at Janice's second wedding.

A few years after Janice married her second husband, Paul, they saw a film that featured an ambiguous female friendship. Although Janice thought the movie fun, Paul went on for days about "perverted lesbians." He claimed that "real women aren't attracted to each other," and that if they are they're dangerous to their kids. "And I should know," huffed Paul. "Who knows women better than a man who's been around?"

The marathon monologue disturbed Janice. She had never told Paul about the weekend with Pam; it was her warm, offbeat, private little memory. Now she was torn. Paul seemed so sure about this. And was Janice really dangerous to their one-year-old daughter?

Janice's happy memory was now a frightening secret. The more anxious she became, the harder it was to put it out of her mind. She began to obsess about the incident and its meaning, and periodically became depressed about it.

That's the first part of the story. Why was Janice letting Paul tell her what was right and wrong? Because he presented a clear, powerful vision on the subject, confident that he knew best. Furthermore, this was a pattern in the rest of their marriage. Paul was the expert on many aspects of Janice's life, such as money, friends, and family. She felt he must be right even when he was ignorant, as he was about women having sex with women.

I learned about this when the couple came to me for sex therapy about a year later, which is the second part of the story. The complaint was Janice's low sex drive. After interviewing them, my diagnosis was, "This isn't a sex problem. It's a relationship problem, an imbalance of power. Janice has no other way of asserting her independence or needs," I told them. "The low desire is also an effective way of avoiding criticism." It was only after a month that Janice revealed her past experience with Pam. As soon as she did, everything made sense.

Janice's dilemma was part of a larger relationship dynamic with Paul. Trying to tidy up your past in order to satisfy someone else's expectations is a common strategy, but it's not a good idea. It leads to resentment or unconscious feelings that are expressed sooner or later.

Contemporary culture promotes rigid ideas about the meaning of the past and our responsibility regarding it:

- ◇ The past is the best predictor of the future.
- ◇ Many things done in the past are unforgivable.
- ◇ Unless people repent, they should be expected to repeat their past behavior.
- ◇ Despite repenting, some people still should not be fully forgiven.
- ◇ It's always easy to know what to do; one can always avoid making mistakes.

What a harsh, cold world such beliefs describe, lacking any sensitivity to the normal ways people change and grow. Most of us go through larger-scale changes, such as adolescent sexual awakenings and mid-life reassessment. We also experience a wide range of gradual, less dramatic, though no less critical, changes that we don't recognize at the time. I hear these changes described in many ways, including, "It stopped being fun," "I began to realize I was actually attractive," "I suppose I outgrew it," and "Maybe I just got tired of the hassles."

Living in a society that refuses to recognize the reality of normal change leads many of us to believe that our past marks us forever. We feel it reflects on who we are *now*, rather than on who we were *then*. A healthier attitude would involve renouncing this belief and accepting the parts of our past we like least, saying, "I wouldn't do that again now, but it was right for me at the time," or "It was the best I could manage."

Our society's belief about an individual's past is, for the most part, hypocritically unforgiving. Pejorative terms like "illegitimate child," "unwed mother," "ex-con," "promiscuous," and "casual abortion" cast people as stereotypes, discrediting their choices and ignoring the human drama behind them.

The government is also guilty of this. The House Un-American Activities Committee, for example, was convened in the 1950s to hound Americans about their beliefs and behavior. The transcripts clearly show Committee members lacked any sense that people change over time.

I suppose we cannot be shocked about such weakness. As *Tristram Shandy* author Laurence Sterne said over a century ago, "Only the brave know how to forgive."

Here's another story about the connection between judging the past and keeping secrets. Note the contrast between the two lovers with a healthy attitude, and their trusted confidants who have more conventional, destructive attitudes.

I caught an episode of a soap opera while delayed in the Seattle airport last year. Don't ask me which soap it was, because they all look alike to me. Jason and Robyn had recently become engaged. Overcome with happiness and feeling very close to Robyn, Jason said he wanted to tell her something.

JASON: Now that we're going to get married, I want to tell you all about me, even stuff from a long time ago. I certainly don't want you to find out certain things from someone else.

ROBYN: Like what?

JASON: Well, when I was in college I was a male stripper. I worked at sororities, bachelorette parties, that sort of thing. It got pretty wild sometimes. I even had a few threesomes. I guess some women think it's a big deal to hang out with entertainers.

ROBYN: You did what?! Jason, that blows my mind! I'm shocked. This doesn't sound like you.

JASON: You're right, I feel embarrassed about it. It made sense at the time, in fact, I even got off on it. But that part of my life is definitely behind me now.

ROBYN: You sure? 'Cause lots of those college girls would still love to, uh, 'hang out' with you now, I bet.

JASON: Hey, don't tease me. Really, it was centuries ago. I just want you. I mean it.

ROBYN: Okay, I love you.

JASON: I love you too. I'm glad I told you.

But in the following two scenes, the "real world" interferes:

JASON: . . . so I told her.

JASON'S ROOMMATE: You what?! That's crazy. She'll never ever let you forget it.

JASON: You don't know Robyn. She's very understanding. And she totally trusts me.

JASON'S ROOMMATE: You don't know women, my friend. You should-n't have told her. She'll be suspicious forever.

ROBYN: . . . so he told me about his "Male Express" days.

ROBYN'S FRIEND: God! So what'd you say?

ROBYN: That it was weird, but since it's obviously behind him, no problem.

ROBYN'S FRIEND: Brave of you to put up a front.

ROBYN: Front? What are you talking about? I meant it.

ROBYN'S FRIEND: Well, you certainly can't trust him now, if that's where he's been. You must have been shattered. You don't really believe he won't be tempted, do you? 'Cause when a man's tempted, that's that.

Jason and Robyn use their relationship as a resource. The way they handle this potential problem brings them closer together. It also helps motivate the next round of sharing and closeness. You can see how the attitude of their "friends," on the other hand, encourages withholding and deception, which frequently results in a mess later on. These friends haven't learned the advice Shakespeare gave in *Othello* over four hundred years ago: "To mourn a mischief that is past and gone is the next way to draw new mischief on."

Guarding the past

One of the easiest ways to keep secrets about the past is simply to lie.

Doesn't this bother people who think of themselves as moral and honest? Well, for some it's awful; for others, it feels regrettable but necessary. Maureen was concerned about HIV and bisexual men when she met Arnold and didn't want to start sleeping with him until they both got tested for the virus. Impatient and unwilling to deal with the issue, Arnold told her that he had never had sexual contact with other men.

"Maureen was all ready to make unfair assumptions," said Arnold, a thirty-eight-year-old architect. "I thought I'd spare us an unnecessary problem, so I justified lying by thinking about the satisfying relationship we were building.

"I only masturbated with a couple of guys a few times," Arnold told me. "Maureen would have insisted it was 'gay sex,' which she felt put her at risk. I felt there was no risk, so I said I'd never done it. I just wanted us to move on and have a normal relationship."

Keeping your past secret may involve destroying evidence, such as mementos. Gifts like paintings or books may need to be given away, particularly if obviously selected by someone whose taste is different from your own.

Recall our discussion about privacy: "I feel okay about this, and simply don't wish to discuss it" is different from "These things are evidence of something 'bad' that I've done."

We may have a distorted sense of what responsibility means. Thus, I periodically hear something like "George refuses to let me wear anything that other men have given me." Why should one person decide the boundaries of permissible privacy for the other? I call this "emotional fascism."

Another way to keep secrets about the past is to allow or encourage a partner's false assumptions. Because doing so does not involve outright lying, those who use this strategy often think they're being "pretty honest." It's a comfortable rationalization, but that's all it is.

The last kind of secret-keeping involves announcing in advance that some behaviors are off-limits. "I don't eat pussy," a man might say, unwilling to examine why he might feel that way. "Call it weird if you like, but that's where I'm at. Subject closed." Here's an example:

Lucy and her fiancé, Krishna, enjoyed sex with each other except for one major issue—he refused to go down on her. Since this was the easiest way for her to have an orgasm, she often felt disappointed. But he always had a good reason for not doing it: His jaw was tired; he had a sore in his mouth; he didn't like her premenstrual smell. Frequently, one or both of them became angry about sex.

Eventually, Lucy confronted Krishna. "I don't think you'll ever go down on me," she yelled. Tired of the game too, Krishna replied, "You're right. I never will. Now that's that. I don't want to discuss it again." He wouldn't explain why, and he had no suggestions as to how Lucy could increase his interest in it.

As I do with most couples, I met individually with Lucy and Krishna the week following our first joint session. Alone with me, Krishna revealed his secret. Years ago he had been fairly clumsy the first time he made love, particularly with his oral technique. Unfortunately, the girl told some of her friends. One of them told her boyfriend, who used the information to humiliate Krishna.

"I like intercourse a lot, but I won't repeat that oral scene," he declared. Why wouldn't he tell Lucy? "She wouldn't understand," he said. "Besides, it's too embarrassing," he offered more accurately. "Listen, this is just the way I am."

And that had become Krishna's theme song: "I'm strange, and I won't communicate about being strange, but this is me. Take it or leave it."

Owning the past

Secrecy about the past comes in a virtually endless variety, in part because of the effective way most of us are taught to criticize our sexuality. In addition, we unwittingly empower our partners to criticize us. But you shouldn't have to defend your past. Your past is part of you, and should be accepted as such.

Trust is an essential part of relationships. Your partner must trust that you have done your best at all times in the past, just as you must trust that your partner has done the same. Only then can intimacy develop.

Be the custodian of your own past (and let others be custodians of theirs). You shouldn't have to ask permission to do the things you already did years ago. You shouldn't have to tolerate a partner relating to the person you **were** rather than to the person you **are.** Practice saying, "Apparently, I had to go through that to get here. If you like me now, you need to accept the whole package."

Just as importantly, tell yourself the same thing—daily, if necessary.

Let us now turn to some examples of sexual secrecy about the past.

"I'd rather Saul think I'm frigid than know I was raped," said Mira, a tall high school administrator. Mira avoided intercourse with Saul because it hurt so much, just as it had with the other two men she'd dated since the rape.

Why did she feel that way? "Because of the way Saul would probably react," she said. "I don't want his pity, and I don't want him wondering if I asked for it. It's just easier to keep it quiet."

"That's true," I replied. Then I asked Mira to consider all the consequences of withholding her painful history. She felt isolated and angry. More importantly, she had compromised the integrity of her sexuality. I quickly added that I wasn't saying she **should** share her past. I felt, however, she needed to be aware of secrecy's true costs, including her current sexual dissatisfaction.

"When the painful intercourse becomes totally unacceptable to you," I said, "sharing this information as part of working through the experience will probably look like a sensible thing to do." The past will then no longer be something that owns Mira. It will simply be what it was: something that happened, "free of irrelevancies and loose ends," as Sir Max Beerbohm once said about the past.

Gary was hiding a different kind of past. The soft-spoken hotel manager didn't quite know how to handle his experiences as a teenager.

"My first sexual encounters," he started after a long sigh, "were with my sister, who seduced me. I have mixed feelings about it—guilt because it was incest, but excitement when I remember how much she enjoyed it. I liked it, too, but I was more concerned about getting caught.

"She was much more mature than I was," he continued. "She was an old sixteen, I was a young fifteen. She talked me into it, saying she needed loving, but that she didn't trust the local boys. Then she wanted to do it again every few weeks. If I said no, she'd pout and say I didn't love her.

"Could a person who started this way have a normal sex life? I'm worried," Gary said in a choked voice. "I almost always date girls the opposite of my sister. She's short, blonde, with small features. So I go for tall, dark, and exotic types. But eventually they all remind me of her. That's when I get anxious, worry about my erection, and stop having sex."

Gary's situation shows how trying to bury the past can actually keep it alive. Whenever Gary makes love, he is emotionally transported to the confusing times of adolescence. And the women he's with become his sister—powerful, seductive, and dangerous.

The message: "I did something bad in the past, which makes me a bad person now." He has no sense that the past and the present are separate, and that the one cannot be judged with the logic, or hindsight, of the other.

Gary needs to decide that he is a normal, acceptable person with power of his own. Accepting his past would be an excellent way to do that. He could then think about how to handle the information with future partners. But **revealing** the secret is not the important thing. **Accepting** it is. Until Gary can do that, he will continue to have sexual difficulty.

Another person hiding past decisions is Colleen. Colleen is unusually articulate about her past. A prostitute before she was seventeen, Colleen told me, "It saved my life. I ran away from insane, brutal parents. Hooking was a way to make a living and feel appreciated. I even finished high school at night.

"But nobody understands that. Well-meaning friends tell me I was a victim, or that my tricks were victims. I'd hear people say that prostitutes are dirty or evil. When I used to respond, 'No, you're wrong,' they'd suspect I was into it, or was encouraging other girls to do it.

"So I don't say anything anymore. I've made up an Aunt Addie who I spent '91 to '95 with. I stick with my story and keep the truth to myself. Wild horses couldn't drag it out of me, because I'm the one who'll get hurt."

Colleen may not feel guilty about the prostitution, but she does carry some baggage from the past. The belief that relationships are temporary, at least for her, reinforces the cruel lessons she learned as a child.

Unfortunately, hiding from judgment and misunderstanding can't help Colleen avoid her internal criticism. That's the voice that says, "Anyone who loves me must be some kind of loser." Colleen believes that if she cares about someone, she'll be left alone. Maintaining silence maintains that belief.

"Why do I mislead people about my past?" she asks rhetorically. "That's easy. People leave if you tell them the truth. Sure, some temporary relationships last longer than others. But what's the bottom line? Some famous guy once said, 'The only difference between blind lust and true love is that lust lasts a little longer.' "

Reclaiming our past is an essential project for each of us. You can do it either by forgiving yourself or by deciding that there's nothing to forgive. Either way, you put the past behind you, which frees up your future. It also redistributes the power in your relationships.

And if we don't do this? Almost half a century ago, Winston Churchill warned, "If we open a quarrel between the past and the present, we shall find that we have lost the future."

Chapter 7

Sexual Secrets:
Deliberate Deception

☉⁄☉

What a tangled web we weave, when first we practice to deceive.

—SIR WALTER SCOTT

Why do we deceive?

There are four reasons that we deliberately deceive others about our sexuality:

1. Deception can be a response to the way we judge our sexuality, our relationships, and ourselves.
2. Deception can be a symbolic statement of other things.
3. Deception can be a way of transferring outdated childhood "truths" into adulthood.
4. Deception can be a way of overcoming our feelings of powerlessness.

Deceiving others almost always creates barriers. These barriers often stand between ourselves and others. They may also prevent us from seeing our own truths.

Because we are typically alienated from sex and our bodies during childhood, it is difficult to accurately evaluate the true nature of our sexuality, or to anticipate how others will react to the truth about us. These distorted perceptions sometimes make the truth look far more dangerous than it really is. Frequently, deception appears necessary when it is not.

Lying comes at a price, and it is almost impossible to overestimate the stress produced by guilt, and the anger it generates in us. We may also underestimate the amount of psychic energy that deception requires, as we diligently monitor our every word and action lest we betray our secrets.

As one sadder-but-wiser client once told me, "One of the nice things about telling the truth is that there's less to remember."

A second reason we deceive is symbolic, more about secret-keeping than about the secret itself. For example, a lie can be a subtle declaration that "No one can control me." Of course, feeling this way doesn't necessarily mean that your partner *wants* to control you. Perhaps it reflects your fear of closeness. Or maybe you are unaware of the amount of compromise required by healthy relationships.

In a similar way, you may use deception as a test. The unconscious dynamic is, "Look how bad I am. Do you still love me?" Another version is, "You say you want to be close to me? I'm going to make it very difficult. Let's see just how much you want to be close." The issue isn't whether or not you get caught in the lie: It's the distance created by the deception that is so powerful.

The third reason we deceive sexually can be called "restimulation." Sometimes we experience old feelings in current situations, which leads us to act in the present as if it were the past.

Children who are constantly criticized or even lovingly scrutinized, for example, learn to conceal anything that matters to them, such as their hobbies, their friends, their dreams, even their school successes. These kids often grow up to be adults who only feel safe when they are hiding. They experience anyone interested in them as intrusive, overwhelming, and frightening. Secrecy often appears to be necessary for surviving adult relationships that feel too much like the dangerous intrusive relationships of youth.

This dynamic may be unintentional. But it can also be deliberate or calculated. Cooper's experience is a good illustration.

Although he started therapy because of career concerns, one day Cooper started talking about sex. That week his girlfriend Sarah had accidentally seen him masturbating for the first time, and observed him rubbing his chest and pinching his nipples. When they made love the next day she repeated the caresses, but he abruptly pushed her away. "Don't touch me that way," he said roughly. "What kind of guy do you think I am?"

Cooper was ashamed that he enjoyed having his nipples stimulated, unaware that many other heterosexual men enjoy this. Although he misled Sarah about it because he was afraid she'd laugh at him, there was a bigger issue: The closeness with her was just too threatening.

Cooper was an only child, born after his mother's second miscarriage. Worried about losing him, too, his parents smothered him with loving concern. To survive their intrusive fussing, Cooper created an inner world of his own, shutting them out with long periods of contented silence.

Long years of self-defense from good intentions led to a necessity for distance to feel safe with his girlfriend. At thirty-three, Cooper is still trying to create a safe childhood for himself by retreating from her well-meaning caresses.

Finally, deliberate deception can also be an expression of powerlessness, a common feeling in many relationships. When we feel appropriately powerful—to be heard, to change the rules, to get appreciation—deception is unnecessary. But there are many ways in which we may feel powerless with a spouse, parent, child, sibling, or close friend. Some thoughts and feelings that express this sense are:

⋄ "I can't seem to get your attention."

⋄ "There seems to be no way to change the rules around here."

⋄ "There seems to be no way to make this relationship more satisfying for me."

⋄ "You said (or implied) that I shouldn't talk about certain things I feel or want to do."

⋄ "I feel coerced into doing this thing that we've already agreed I don't want to do."

Such feelings can lead to deception—that is, breaking one or more parts of a relationship contract—if we feel that staying within the contract's bounds doesn't work anymore. While deceiving someone may look like an act of defiance or the assertion of power, it may actually be an act of fear, desperation, or frustration.

Mick was a salesman who was struggling to stay in his fourteen-year marriage. His wife, Tara, was always depressed. She couldn't handle housework, and she didn't want a job. Worse still, she didn't want to discuss Mick's unhappiness.

"I love her, and want to stay with her," he said sadly, "but she just refuses to make an effort. What am I supposed to do? Talking doesn't work. Nagging doesn't work. Pleading, threatening, and ignoring her don't work either."

Eventually, Mick started sleeping with a client he saw from time to time. A classic "I'll-do-anything-I-want" move? I don't think so. "I felt totally boxed in," Mick told me soon after the affair started. "I hated where I was and saw no way out. Tara said she had no energy for my 'demands.' I had to have physical contact with someone, so I let it happen. I feel like a person again. And, of course, guilty as hell."

Mick, I'm certain, would rather be talking, laughing, and making love with his wife. But he feels totally powerless to arrange that. And since Tara refuses to get either individual or marital counseling, there isn't much that can be done to heal the situation.

How do we feel about deception? How do you?

Most people experience two different kinds of feelings about their deception. One is short-term and self-centered, almost childlike:

⋄ "I'm glad I'm doing this"
⋄ "It's about time I stood up to her/him."
⋄ "Finally, I'm doing something for me."
⋄ "I'm not responsible, because I've been pushed to this."
⋄ "I have to do this; I have no choice."
⋄ "I deserve this, and I refuse to feel guilty about it."

I believe another, more complex set of feelings lies beneath. While some say they are completely unaffected by deceiving their intimates, I don't think this is true. In fact, the denial and blame behind such statements are part of the secrecy experience. We must do something, psychologically, to normalize our deception—that is, to deflect our guilt, shame, and self-criticism.

Somewhere in our psyches, almost everyone seems to have the sense that deceiving a significant other is wrong. Is it ethics—or the memory of having been deceived ourselves? You can surely recall how you felt when you discovered yourself deceived: betrayed, humiliated, ashamed, angry. Although we may not think about these feelings and experiences often, they lurk in the mind's shadows, whispering.

So secret-keepers have a conflict. The child-like self says deception is necessary, while the more adult self condemns it. The clash between these two sets of feelings frequently results in depression or anger. The depression leads to isolation, while the anger leads to blame.

In either case, the result is generally an adversarial relationship, culminating in feelings like "It's me against you," or "Either you're the problem or I'm the problem." This adversarial dynamic is a wound that must be healed before any other change can occur. Unfortunately, we usually try to solve our problems without addressing the pain of being adversaries first. Such efforts typically succeed only at great cost, if at all. Sometimes they make the problem worse.

Acknowledging this win-lose attitude is important for two reasons. First, it helps us look at inner conflicts about our own behavior. Second, it creates the possibility of change that is more than cosmetic or temporary. Allowing an adversarial relationship to continue is to let the seeds of future bitterness lie in the ground, germinating.

Beneath both the childish and the parental feelings about deception is a pretense of powerlessness. As the deceiver, we are convinced we acted out of necessity: "I was pushed to it, I had to have the gratification," while the voice of guilt and shame says, "I'm a bad person, too weak to resist."

But you *can* see deception differently—as active, rather than reactive.

The active nature of deception

While it is usually easy to see another's deception as a subtle form of control or power, it is much harder to see our own deceptions that way. It is, however, important to realize that deception is a **choice**, and to take responsibility for that choice.

Doing so can help you deal with deception's consequences, both intended and unintended. Furthermore, because taking responsibility is an act of reclaiming your power, it can also help expand the range of options you perceive in a given situation.

Deception is an active choice in several other ways. For example, deception frequently maintains a relationship's status quo by making it more bearable. Thus, if the relationship survives the early stages of deception, the system normally becomes more stable, not less. A predictable dance of deception develops, in which all participants know their roles.

The system is also more stable because of a strange kind of accommodation. Deception can stretch a relationship to create possibilities not otherwise available. An example is a rule that frustrates you ("Don't do it") combined with an activity that satisfies you ("I'm doing it"). The combination often proves irresistible, although costly in the long run.

Deception, and the denial and blame that comes with it, prevents people from identifying and healing the real problems that exist between them. Everyone considering secrecy needs to acknowledge this as part of their decision-making.

Deception is a dynamic tool of evolution, modifying any relationship it touches. Several of the following scenarios typically occur:

- ◇ You're not present and involved in quite the way you appear to be.
- ◇ You cannot fully share yourself.
- ◇ You're on guard.
- ◇ Your partner, in some ways, becomes the enemy.
- ◇ The scope of a shared vision for the future is reduced.
- ◇ Resources are being drained, instead of being multiplied through collaboration.
- ◇ You are creating the relationship's future primarily on your own, instead of jointly creating it with your partner.

⟡ The relationship may now include a third party. Whether it does or not, the deception itself is a third party in the relationship, the same as alcohol, overwork, or compulsive gambling can be.

Those being deceived often say that the most damning part is being unaware of participating in this new, revised relationship. Needless to say, these partners haven't given permission for the change.

Why don't we acknowledge the active nature of deception? Perhaps it's our hesitation to take responsibility for risky or ethically questionable behavior.

The relationship contract

So too, deception isn't simply imposed by one person on another. It's imposed by one person on a relationship. Deception specifically excludes your partner from efforts to solve a problem or nurture yourself. This is exactly the opposite of intimacy, particularly when your need for support arises from the partner or the relationship itself.

We've already discussed relationship "contracts" several times. They are the agreements, frequently unspoken, that two people make about acceptable behavior, and the penalties for unacceptable behavior.

Deception almost always violates a relationship contract. How?

⟡ It involves "forbidden" behavior. An example is the use of birth control pills after agreeing not to.

⟡ Deception itself is typically prohibited behavior, regardless of the content of the deception. An example could be something as seemingly harmless as kissing a co-worker at her office birthday party, and then denying it later.

Most people do not break their agreements lightly. Why, then, do so many of us violate our relationship contracts periodically?

⬦ **Indifference:** We don't care about the relationship or contract.

⬦ **Denial:** We deny that our behavior is truly a violation of our agreement.

⬦ **Enmity:** Consciously or not, we feel that our partner is an adversary.

⬦ **Powerlessness:** We don't realize we have enough power to get what we want in other ways.

⬦ **Fear:** We're afraid that the consequences of not deceiving will be even worse.

Wherever there is intimacy, or the desire for it, there is also fear of commitment. Our fear tempts us, consciously or not, to deceive as a way of creating a boundary or barrier between ourselves and others, especially our beloved.

Why do we decide to deceive?

Let's look at some common subjects of deception.

EXTRAMARITAL SEX

The most talked-about deception, and the one that causes substantial relationship problems, is extramarital sex.

Surveys by *Psychology Today*, *Cosmopolitan*, and *Playboy* suggest that "affairs" occur in at least half of American marriages. Comedian Jackie Mason has an even higher estimate: "Three-quarters of today's men cheat in America," he says. "The rest go to Europe."

The results of magazine surveys contrast sharply with the results of opinion surveys, such as the California Poll. When asked what contributes most to a successful marriage, the answer most often given was "sexual fidelity."

How can we account for this contrast? Which contrast? Well, why are so many people willing to invest the time and energy necessary to deceive their partners in this way when there is a general consensus that doing so is wrong? We might also ask the question in another way: If affairs are so common, why are they formally condemned by almost everyone?

In her book *The Extramarital Connection*, Lynn Atwater suggests that, "We are sexual schizophrenics. We say one thing and do another. We are still emotionally attached to traditional beliefs of sexual exclusivity, while we live with the needs and desires provoked by contemporary values which hold sexual expression to be a new social frontier."

I believe she is right. Our traditions about exclusivity date from an era of short marriages (due to short lives), rigid gender roles, and almost no privacy or personal time. We have yet to adjust our ideas to the modern reality of long life (which leads to long marriages), more flexible social options, and extraordinary amounts of personal space and time.

Approaching the issue psychologically, we can see the clandestine relationship as a perfect recapitulation of childhood's drama. The person having an affair is, symbolically, hiding a treasure from Mommy or Daddy. The secret affair repeats the exciting, dangerous secret of childhood sexuality that we concealed so well from our parents. This helps explain why affairs are so universally condemned, and yet still enjoyed.

But this is only part of the explanation. Other contemporary reasons for the high incidence of extramarital affairs include:

1. The expectation of personal fulfillment. As Judith Bardwick notes in *In Transition*, the idea that people should be personally fulfilled, beyond seeing their families grow and serving their God, is new and radical. In fact, we really don't know yet if widespread "happiness" is possible over a long period of time. Frequently, an extramarital affair is part of the search for that elusive fulfillment. Typically, however, the search for peace of mind is more effective when directed internally rather than externally.

2. Our exaggerated notions of sexual satisfaction. Until a century ago, very few people spoke openly about sex, and there were few sexually explicit materials available to common folks. The modern accessibility of sexual information and artistic expression is cause for celebration, but we should also be aware of its disadvantages.

One is the exaggerated picture that's being conveyed about "great sex." Magazines, movies, literature, well-meaning gossip, X-rated materials, the internet, and even some self-help books have given us the notion that if we find the right partner, we can have the ecstasy of endless multiple simultaneous effortless orgasms.

In reality, sex under the best circumstances is relatively brief, somewhat repetitive, and rarely mind-boggling.

3. The cultural norm that nonmarital sex is better. One of the startling things that *Playboy* did three decades ago was formalize and promote the idea that wives were boring. Times have changed since then, of course. Magazines and TV now tell us that husbands are boring too.

The usual media portrayal of marital sexuality ranges from perfunctory to nonexistent. Less than 10 percent of the sex presented on television, for example, takes place between married people. The exciting sex in romance novels is generally between women (married or not) and strangers.

A natural result of this is that people turn to other lovers. Comedian

Buddy Hackett best represents this position when he says that if you want to read about marriage and good sex, you have to buy two different books.

4. *The routinization of marital sex.* Habituation is inevitable in long-term relationships. Routinization, however, is not. Consider the way most people prepare for sex with a nonspouse. The special underwear, perfume, teasing, little notes, setting aside time, and anticipation enrich extramarital sex tremendously.

This kind of attention would improve the sex in almost anyone's marriage, making an affair seem much less "necessary." Those who do not wish to make this investment always have "good" reasons to believe it would be fruitless. Often, the true reason is that they don't *want* to increase the intimacy in their marriage.

5. *The modern commitment to career.* Time was when most paid jobs were dirty, tiring, and even dangerous. Today's careers are different. While work is still tiring, many of us also expect it to be stimulating, rewarding, and a vehicle for self-expression. Thus, many of us today give our best thinking, sharing, listening, and creativity to our colleagues, who are busy doing the same. In some ways, many of us are now at our most attractive at work, rather than at home.

Our co-workers also seem to understand our concerns and our language better than our mates. When we add the fact that workplaces are now mixed-gender, we can understand how many affairs get started.

A final note on affairs

Perhaps you're wondering why this book has no separate chapter on extramarital affairs. It's because affairs are just like other secrets; they are primarily an expression of feelings about ourselves or our relationships. Many affairs are about attachment and distance rather than sex.

True, affairs are a way for some people with low-desire spouses to have more sex. But frequently, the men and women involved report that the lovemaking at home is not that bad.

Of course, we know that "fidelity" refers to much more than sex. In fact, an intimate conversation can be far more of an infidelity than physical lovemaking would be. So this book treats affairs like any other secret. There is no separate chapter on affairs because affairs are rarely a separate chapter in our lives. They are, more commonly, part of a theme woven through the special book we each write during our lifetime.

FAKING ORGASMS

Why do women fake orgasms? First we must understand why they don't have orgasms. One reason is inner conflict about sex. Having been taught to be "good girls" (non-sexual), adult women often have difficulty finally letting go and surrendering to their sexual feelings. As sociologist Carol Cassell says, it helps if you can claim you were "swept away" by true love, for example, or alcohol.

The second barrier to having orgasms is performance pressure, fostered by the belief that orgasm proves a woman's sexual competence. The third reason is the myth that women should come from intercourse. Yes, it is a myth. Less than half of American women can come from intercourse alone.

But why should women who don't come fake it? For the most part, they do it to satisfy their partners. As Shere Hite reported in her follow-up survey of seven thousand men, "The overwhelming majority of men realized that women often did not orgasm during intercourse, and found this a source of pressure. Many felt it was their fault." That's why men so often pressure women by asking, "Didja come?"

A few men also fake orgasms. I remember one friend's college experience. After a party he talked a young woman into bed with him, but decided about halfway through that it was a mistake. Instead of discussing things with her, he simply pretended that he was satisfied rather quickly, and followed with a hasty exit.

Faking an erection, of course, is quite difficult, but some men with chronic problems do act surprised when they don't get a hard-on or when they get one and lose it almost immediately. For some men, feigning shock is easier than talking about the problem honestly.

STDs (Sexually Transmitted Diseases)

No one used to inquire about the genital health or sexual history of a partner; it was considered unnecessary and unromantic. Because of the AIDS, herpes, warts, and chlamydia epidemics, however, it is now necessary (although still, unfortunately, considered unromantic) to ask questions. But many still don't. Hope has always been a popular approach to contraception and protection. But it fails as preventive medicine as much as it always has as a contraceptive.

Unfortunately, you may not get an honest or dependable answer even if you do ask. Some people don't really know if they have, or have been exposed to, anything. Worse, some people do know, and are unwilling to tarnish their sexual attractiveness with the truth. They don't bring up the subject, and if you do, they lie.

Unless you get tested together and agree to share the results, there is no easy way of knowing how much you should rely on a partner's description of his or her sexual health. Only real familiarity, the kind that requires lots of time together, can provide a few helpful clues. But some STDs show no visible symptoms. Until you develop that closeness with a new friend, you might want to trust a condom instead, or limit your relationship to mutual masturbation or tennis.

SAME-SEX EXPERIMENTATION

According to sexologists Moser and Morin, most true bisexuals are comfortable with their orientation. But some heterosexuals who have had a same-sex fling or two are troubled about theirs. Believing (correctly) that they're straight, they have trouble integrating these other experiences. They're afraid they're bi or, worse, "latent homo." Partly to deny this fear, they lie about themselves.

These people don't know what the Kinsey study found, and what countless surveys confirm: Almost half of American men and almost a quarter of American women have at least one same-sex experience as adults. Almost all think of themselves as heterosexual.

DISLIKE

"I don't like the way you touch me or make love." I believe this is such a crucial piece of information that anything other than saying it plainly and clearly counts as deliberate deception. Do you fall into this category? For a refresher on the subject, see Chapter 4 on arousal and response.

SEXUAL APPETITE

Western culture has traditionally pretended that women dislike and thus avoid sex, and that men are always interested in it. This belief is alive and well in modern America:

A man wakes his wife at 3 A.M., saying, "I brought you two aspirin and a glass of water." "For what?" demands his sleepy spouse. "For your headache," he replies. "You're crazy," she says, "I don't have a headache." "Finally!" exclaims her husband. "Now we can make love."

To get a clear picture of the imbalanced expectations this joke presents, read it again with the wife waking the husband. In our culture, that version wouldn't be considered funny.

With these images so clearly defined, it is tempting to conceal our level of sexual interest if it runs counter to stereotype. Fearing criticism, some women conceal a hearty sexual appetite. Some men, on the other hand, try to hide their relatively low sex drive, often with excuses or nit-picking.

We deceive our lovers this way because we believe there is a "right" or "normal" level of sexual desire. But normal desire isn't a specific amount, it's a *range*. And it's a much wider range than most of us realize. If you are not comfortable with your sexual appetite, you can productively seek help to change it. You should know that most people who enter therapy with desire problems are normal.

Another reason we deceive each other about our desire is because we're afraid of rejection. As we have already seen, this is usually based on a lack of self-acceptance. Those who really accept themselves rarely worry about the dangers of being honest with others.

A woman who feels her libido is abnormally low, for example, may disguise this during courtship for fear of discouraging suitors. After marriage, she feels safer revealing her true interest level, which may clash with her husband's. When the couple routinely fights about sex, she can feel justified in her deception: "I knew sex would be a problem if I told the truth."

How much is absolutely too little desire? According to Joan Rivers, it's if you go so long without sex that you forget who ties up who. Too much desire? It's if you die of malnutrition because you don't stop making love long enough to eat once a day.

SEX WITH A TABOO PARTNER

As we have already seen, not all secrets are kept from a spouse or lover. Some are kept from friends and relatives. Consider the taboo partner: the sister, friend, son, ex-husband, rabbi, etc., of someone you know. We keep the relationship secret because we imagine terrible consequences from telling the truth. This may be a rational judgment. Then again, it may be the Secrecy Imperative's distortion.

We could avoid a lot of trouble with some straight talk. A woman might say, "Dad, your golf partner has asked me out and I just wanted to tell you myself before you heard it through the grapevine." Or your friend might say, "Serena, I know you're close to your brother's ex-wife. I'd like to start seeing her, and figured we ought to discuss it first." This is *not* the kind of grown-up conversation you hear on TV.

It would be interesting, in passing, to look at why we get involved with taboo partners in the first place. For some, the taboo itself is attractive. Consciously or not, the behavior says, "I can do whatever I like. I won't let logic or others' feelings stop me from seeing anybody I want."

Risky or forbidden relationships are sometimes used for other, often unconscious purposes as well. These include expressing revenge, anger, or sadness. Sometimes the desired result is disrupting the relationship that your new partner is having with a roommate, ex-lover, or co-worker.

Finally, some use taboo partners to create the next chapter in the ongoing script of "Love Never Works Out For Me." I'm delighted to tell the story of a patient who just recently interrupted such a pattern.

Twenty-eight-year-old Ron had been in therapy about a month. He was depressed, had little self-confidence, and no women friends. "Oh, Juanita asked me out today," he said one afternoon. "That's my brother's ex-wife. We've been friends for years. I'm not sure she's really done with him, but she says she is. It would be nice to make out and cuddle with her. She's really nice."

But the more Ron talked, the more Juanita looked like an accident just waiting to happen. She had started to call him at work almost every day, chatting casually even when he said he was busy. She mentioned fantasizing about them getting married. She wanted to be happy again, "like I was with Bruce."

I asked Ron what he intended to do. "Well, I hate to keep secrets from my family, but I don't think anyone would understand. I'll have to keep this quiet for a while." And what were his plans? Did he see himself marrying her. "No, I don't think she's right for me. Besides, the family gatherings would be really awkward."

I had Ron fantasize what it would be like: How would he feel deceiving his brother, and later, ending the romance with Juanita when he met someone more eligible for marriage? Neither felt very good. "But what can I do?" Ron asked.

We approached it from another direction. "If the future consequences of a current decision look unacceptable, decide there are alternatives—and then find them," I said. Ron was intrigued. "You mean this could be a mess that I can actually avoid!" he said excitedly. It's a concept he already understood about work, but not about love.

Ron realized he didn't have to be a person whose romances never worked out. Instead, he became a person who chose his romances carefully, so they had a good chance of being satisfying.

Let's mention a few other common deceptions that are a little smaller in scope. How many of these do you keep from your mate?

◇ I like to touch your underwear when you're not around.
◇ I like to wear your underwear when you're not around.
◇ I like the noise you make during sex.
◇ I masturbate looking at your picture or thinking about you.

⟡ Sometimes I imagine we're teenage siblings.

⟡ I wonder if I'm normal (and maybe even think that **that's** not normal).

Perhaps you deceive friends or others with some of these:

⟡ I love being held down during sex.

⟡ I imagine you're a better lover than I am.

⟡ I don't really have much sexual experience.

⟡ I make wild sounds when I come.

⟡ I have no interest in women other than my wife (men rarely admit this to each other).

Now that we understand the conflicting feelings that often accompany deception, we know that we frequently handle this conflict by pushing away our lovers. Thus, deception often creates situations that demand further deception, demanding that we relinquish our personal power.

In the next section, we'll look at the process of decision-making. Everyone wants to make decisions that lead to happiness and closeness. Let's turn now to how we accept ourselves, setting us firmly on the path of more satisfying sex.

Chapter 8

Accepting Yourself—and Taking a Chance

❧

Though I am not naturally honest, I am so sometimes by chance.

—WILLIAM SHAKESPEARE

This is the chapter in which you will explore the nuts and bolts of sexual honesty. It will help you make intelligent decisions about the level of honesty you desire—and how to accomplish that.

Most decisions about sexual honesty and withholding are not carefully thought through. As discussed in Chapters 2 and 3, secrecy often develops unconsciously, appearing in adult relationships uninvited. When secrecy is chosen consciously, it is frequently a response to some kind of fear.

Either way, you may now be considering a change. Perhaps you now understand the consequences of your silence in a new way; perhaps you see the benefits of openness and honesty more clearly. Maybe your needs have changed since you last thought about these issues, and it's time to update your relationship assumptions and decision-making.

Choosing to be more sexually forthcoming makes sense when you have good reasons for doing so, and have developed the personal resources to handle the results. Let's look at each of these.

What's the point of sharing?

When people in unhealthy relationships feel angry, scared, confused, humiliated, sad, or lonely, they often express this through hostility or manipulation. Healthy relationships provide healthy alternatives for expressing these feelings. When partners in good relationships do talk directly about their feelings, they expect to be heard. For many people, this is a radical concept.

Being honest isn't something you do *to* someone. Rather, it is something you do **with** someone, enhancing intimacy or self-esteem. But this can be tricky. For example, the following disclosures would, in most circumstances, be hostile:

- ⋄ "I think of your sister when we make love."
- ⋄ "I had much better orgasms with that one-night stand last year."
- ⋄ "Mom, let me tell you all the details about having sex with my boyfriend."
- ⋄ "Before you leave me, I want you to know that I've been having an affair."

Now, some constructive aspects of sexual honesty:

- ⋄ The sharing specifically addresses the effects of secrecy on you and/or the relationship.
- ⋄ The sharing doesn't manipulate or mislead your partner.
- ⋄ The sharing contributes positively to your health and/or the relationship.

From this list, we can decide that the following are good reasons for sexual honesty. When you share in good faith, under the right circumstances, the goals below are possible and healthy:

⋄ Get closer to your partner.

⋄ Improve your sexual relationship and sexual experience.

⋄ Increase your self-esteem.

⋄ Reduce the physical or emotional stresses of secrecy.

⋄ Change a relationship, or support a current change.

Let's look at these in more detail.

GET CLOSER

Sharing can bring two people closer by helping them understand each other. True, your partner may disagree with your perceptions, be disappointed by your feelings, or not want to give you what you want. At the very least, however, he or she will have a better sense of what the world looks like through your eyes.

Sharing can provide "the missing link." As one man told me about his wife's sharing, "I didn't like what I heard, but I was glad I heard it. Even though I don't know what to do about it, at least now I know why she avoided making love."

Even if sharing only lets a partner know you feel ashamed or angry, it can still make a difference. You may not see the positive effects right away, but they will appear eventually. The changes may not even appear in a sexual context, but rather in a related area, such as the balance of power within the relationship, the way you talk to each other, or just the way you feel when you're together.

When you share strong feelings and emotional experiences, even painful ones, you and your lover may very well become closer. You may, for example, feel the exhilaration of taking risks by revealing yourself, or you may think about your relationship in new ways. You may feel the excitement of having your private desires greeted and accepted, or you may feel the pleasure of seeing your partner's emerging self-esteem.

Sometimes revealing yourself involves sharing pain. You may feel sad about having kept part of yourself hidden. You may even feel ashamed or embarrassed. At the same time, sharing the secret may also include recognizing your lover's pain. He or she will probably feel bad about having been deceived, or about having encouraged the deception unknowingly.

Finally, sharing can also include a mutual acknowledgment that this is a moment of transition. You and your partner may feel proud of your relationship. You may appreciate its resources, or you may both worry that more change is coming, fearing that it will be difficult to handle.

In all these ways, the strong emotions surrounding self-disclosure can bring lovers closer together. Whether it's a devastating tornado or a million-dollar lottery win, powerful experiences always offer this opportunity.

MAKE SEX MORE SATISFYING

The desire to improve your sexual relationship is another good reason to be honest about your sexual desires, fantasies, and experiences. Some people find that honesty comes fairly easily to them, while others find it so difficult that they resort to it only out of desperation.

You may decide to share only after enduring unsatisfying sex for a long time. Or you may feel relatively satisfied, but discover or decide that more is possible. Sometimes we desire change after learning more about ourselves. Many therapists, for example, suggest masturbation as an excellent way for women to learn more about their sexual responsiveness. Women who have never come before often have their first orgasm in this way, opening the door for further exploration with a partner.

Sexual honesty can lead to better sex simply by allowing us to be more relaxed. Remember "lights-out" Sandy from Chapter 4? Telling men that she is embarrassed about her body could change her sexual experiences dramatically. Lovemaking might no longer be a place where Sandy punished herself. Her partners just might appreciate her body and give her positive feedback. She could be less self-conscious and more relaxed.

And, of course, sharing information with lovers gives them a chance to stimulate us the way we like. A man ashamed of wanting his butt caressed, for instance, might finally get to enjoy this experience, noting that his partner is perfectly willing to do it. But if he doesn't ask, he almost guarantees that he'll miss out on a desired sensation.

Happily, self-revelation is rarely completely one-sided. Your sharing often invites your partner to share, bringing them benefits, too. Irv and Peg, an older couple I worked with years ago, were retired professors who enjoyed their marriage and led active lives. They came to me for advice on several issues concerning their adult children and adolescent grandchildren.

Our session had an easy, comfortable feeling. At one point I gave Peg a few of my magazine articles to share with her daughter. The following session she looked more serious than usual.

"Irv, one of these articles got me thinking," she announced after we all sat down. "I know you love me and want to give me pleasure in bed, but it's time to tell you that sexually, I've changed. A big, hard penis banging into me just isn't my first choice anymore."

Irv's face was a mixture of worry, affection, and excitement. "You mean I don't have to do the old battering ram routine all the time? That's great!" he said, to Peg's surprise. "I'm not as young as I once was either, you know." Her honesty had encouraged his.

As they realized they'd each been accommodating what they *assumed* the other wanted, they began laughing. The truth is, intercourse had become hard work for each of them. They both preferred hand or mouth stimulation. But Peg didn't want to hurt Irv's pride as a lover, and Irv didn't want Peg to feel she didn't turn him on anymore. So they kept quiet and struggled, ironically, out of loving consideration for each other's feelings.

"Now let's not forget intercourse altogether, right?" Peg said playfully. Irv winked and nodded. If only all my therapy sessions were this satisfying, I thought.

Sometimes sharing enables you to satisfy your partner more. Take Lila and James, a fundamentalist Christian couple. They enjoyed their lovemaking together, but each admitted to me individually, in private, that it lacked a spark.

Lila was disappointed about several things, one of which was that she never had a chance to give James oral sex. "Have you ever suggested it?" I asked in our individual session. "No," she replied, "he's real Bible-minded. I'm afraid he'd think I'm a loose woman, and wonder about my past."

Privately, James also expressed disappointment. "Lila's very loving, very giving," he said, "but I sure wish she'd go down on me." Surprise! I inquired if James had ever encouraged Lila, or asked her about oral sex. "No way," he said with feeling. "I wouldn't take a chance on offending her. She might not understand that it's a common, normal thing to do."

To start their joint session the following week, I opened with, "Many mates keep secrets about sex from each other. While privacy is crucial in relationships, some secrecy is unnecessary, even harmful. I never force anyone to reveal information, but if either of you wants to share anything with each other, now is a good time."

The room was quiet. Then Lila turned to James and spoke. "I don't feel totally free," she said, "I'd like to . . ." She paused. "I'd like to please you in **different** ways." The words didn't come easily for Lila. She was frightened, but finally managed to tell him, despite her reservations. When James realized what Lila was offering, he was delighted. Lila was moved by her husband's acceptance. It was a great example of a win-win situation. As our work progressed, they admitted several other things to each other. With growing delight they began to realize that each was more open-minded than the other had thought.

INCREASE SELF-ESTEEM

Enhancing or supporting self-esteem is another good reason to share information. In a healthy partnership, each person is vitally interested in the self-esteem of the other. Honesty makes good use of the partnership's resources.

Self-esteem is the sense of accepting yourself, regardless of what you do. And it does not come easily to everyone. Low self-esteem has its roots in early childhood, when we first experience our parents' criticism and appreciation.

Children need to understand that although they may do unacceptable things, they themselves are acceptable people. This acceptance leads to a deep sense that "I am okay." But as Swiss psychologist Alice Miller notes, many parents tend to criticize children in terms of who they *are,* rather than in terms of what they *do.*

How many times have you heard a parent say, "You're a bad girl," instead of saying, "When you don't pay attention, it's easy to knock over your milk. You must pay attention." Or "Nice boys don't touch themselves," instead of "I know that feels good, but please don't touch your penis in public. Let's wait until we get home, and you can do that in your room."

So most children learn the damaging lesson that if they *do* something bad, they *are* bad. They also learn (from parents who are otherwise quite loving) that they are "lazy," "sloppy," "naughty," and so on, instead of learning that they are wonderful little people who sometimes do inconvenient, incorrect, or self-defeating things.

People who manage to develop high self-esteem have been able to separate themselves just a bit from their victories and defeats. They may not like something they do, but they don't see this as a reason to stop liking themselves. And they don't exaggerate their successes, because their sense of self isn't based on individual accomplishments.

A healthy level of self-disclosure is an expression of self-acceptance, and thus of self-esteem. For example, sharing can help you maintain or strengthen your self-image as an honest person. This might be important after a particular event, or as part of a current growth process.

My neighbor Tom told me a great story about this once. "I've always believed myself to be pretty honest," he said, "More so than a lot of guys. One day my six-year-old asks me what a 'white lie' is. As I was telling him, I realized I'd been holding out on Rae [his wife] for weeks. I didn't like the new way she'd been kissing me lately. I decided to tell her that very night. As a result, we had a great talk about a whole bunch of stuff."

For some people the stakes are much higher, which they often describe as "no longer wanting to live a lie." A man may finally tell his wife that he sometimes wears women's clothes. A woman may admit to her husband that she was sterilized before they met. For many, the exciting sense of self-acceptance following the disclosure outweighs the difficulties honesty can bring.

Other secrets may appear relatively minor to outsiders, but have strong meaning for the person involved. "Coming out" might include dressing so that a small bosom is no longer disguised; refusing to allow a lover's cat in the room during sex; and acknowledging having seen and enjoyed X-rated films.

Perhaps you've kept one or more sexual secrets because in the past your partner reacted to the truth harshly. (We're talking about experience here, not just assumptions.) Sharing information can support your decision to stop shying away from confrontation—which can have a dramatic impact on your self-esteem. Examples of assertive sharing might include:

⋄ I don't come from intercourse. I'd like to talk about what does make me come.

⋄ I want to date other people.

⋄ I'd like to go down on you. I'd love it if you'd go down on me.

⋄ I enjoy watching erotic videos when I masturbate.

⋄ I use Viagra.

⋄ I don't feel masturbation is a betrayal of our marriage.

⋄ I want to end this relationship.

One thing I've told clients over the years is, "Once you decide that avoiding pain is your primary goal, you never get to make another decision." Avoiding confrontation is a full-time, emotionally costly job. Everything else becomes subordinated to it, requiring you to mind-read and play perpetual catch-up. Deciding to end the whole exhausting routine is a big boost to self-esteem.

Honesty also increases self-esteem in its inherent statement that "I am an equal." Many people live with imbalanced power arrangements, unaware that relationships can function any other way—or that change is even possible. Sharing can be a powerful intervention in an otherwise unyielding situation.

The idea that what you want is as important as what your partner, parent, or child wants may be a radical, life-changing concept. It can rebalance the power in a relationship. Of course, this involves assuming responsibility for your own dissatisfaction, rather than blaming it on someone or something more powerful than you are. That can be both frightening and exhilarating.

REDUCE THE STRESSES OF SECRECY

Honesty is an important way to reduce the physical and emotional burdens imposed on us by secrecy. Nothing illustrates this point better than the story of a client I worked with a little over ten years ago.

Aaron was referred to me by a colleague at the University Sleep Clinic. He was having nightmares about twice a week, always with the same theme. "I'm so tired of being chased," the thirty-one-year-old father told me. "Sometimes it's by Nazis, other times by escaped convicts or the police. I always wake up running for my life."

I asked Aaron about his family, job, and overall health, and gave him my intake form to complete. In response to the last question: "In one word, please describe your sexual relationships." Aaron's answer was "schizophrenic."

"It's great when I masturbate," he replied when I asked about this. "I have super fantasies about old girlfriends, and I last a long time. But with my wife it's sort of dull. And I pretend to be more interested than I really am."

Considered separately, Aaron's answer and the recurring nightmares could have signaled many different things. But taken together, I wondered if they reflected the stress of an internal conflict. I asked Aaron to tell me more about his hidden sexual arrangement.

"Well, I don't like hiding," he said sadly, "or feeling like two different people." I asked how much he thought about getting caught. "I used to think about it a lot," said Aaron, "especially after I heard a radio show one night. A caller said that wives could always tell when their husbands were unfaithful." An interesting way to describe his secret life, I thought.

"I've just trained myself never to think about it," Aaron continued with a sigh of resignation. "I just enjoy what I've got and try to stay out of trouble."

I believe it's virtually impossible for our minds to ignore strong feelings over the course of time. Aaron's nightmares were starting to look like the product of repressed fear and guilt. "What do you think would happen if you simply told Beth about your 'other life'?" I asked. Aaron shuddered. "I couldn't," he said simply. "Besides, why would I admit something like that?"

It took a few sessions, but I finally helped Aaron understand that masturbating was not bad, "even though" he was married. And I explained that wild fantasies are common. "Perhaps," I suggested, "your wife might be willing to go with you to counseling so that both of you can be more sexually fulfilled."

Aaron wasn't ready for this, so we continued individual counseling. I remember him saying, about a month later, that "Our talks about what's normal have given me a lot to think about." Several weeks later, Aaron said, "You know, I'm feeling such relief from our sessions. I didn't realize how uptight the whole thing made me. Oh, by the way," he added as our session ended, "the nightmares have just about stopped."

Although Aaron did not tell his wife the truth about his sexuality, he had eventually come to accept it himself. For Aaron, that was enough. He looked more secure and self-confident as he went to the door. His life had changed forever.

CREATE OR MAINTAIN RELATIONSHIP CHANGE

Honest sharing can be a way of creating change in your relationship, and it can unfold in different ways. Winston, for example, was a construction worker who drank heavily. As soon as he came home from work he opened a six-pack of beer "to relax." By half-past eight he was usually asleep on the living room couch, six empty cans beside him. He and his wife Julie had practically no life together, and rarely enjoyed each other's company.

Julie had left him and returned twice. To complicate matters, they had an infant daughter. Winston refused to discuss his drinking at home or in our session, insisting he wasn't an alcoholic because he could quit anytime. Julie's pleas for a warmer relationship fell on deaf ears. Desperate for a solution, Julie chose to force the issue by confronting Winston's self-image. She brought a twelve-month wall calendar to our session, with three days circled in red.

"These are the three times we've made love this year," she announced brandishing the calendar, "and it's already October. We never have sex because you're either drunk or asleep. I've had two offers of affairs from men at work, and I'm considering which one to accept. Are you going to change and save our marriage, or shall we get a divorce?"

Winston accused her of bluffing, then of not understanding him, and finally of being a slut. "I read an article that says most couples under thirty have sex at least once a week," Julie countered. "Are you going to get normal or not?"

As Julie feared, Winston refused to acknowledge her pain, refused to recognize his role in the disintegration of their marriage, and refused to bond with her to save their family. But she finally had enough information, and was able to act. It was time for her to make the biggest change of all: separation and divorce. "It was the hardest thing I've ever done," she told me a year later, "but I've never regretted it."

Sometimes sharing leads to change that is just as drastic, but with a very different result.

A bookkeeper I worked with felt powerless in her relationship, which all her friends believed was perfect. While Dawn was periodically able to tell her girlfriend Giselle that she was unhappy, somehow change never followed.

Dawn eventually decided to use the issue of sex to make Giselle understand her frustration. "We always do it the same way—your way," she complained. "Always you on top, never me. Why can't we ever switch positions or experiment?" she demanded. "I am very unhappy sexually. Did you know that?" Dawn had finally dropped the bomb.

"What's the difference what position we use?" Giselle replied. "You usually come, I have a good enough time, why do we have to mess around with things?" Dawn's face sagged as she met Giselle's resistance. "I don't know what to say," she said to me, near tears. "She's right, as usual. Is there something wrong with me?"

I encouraged them to talk to each other more, but they kept returning to the same place, so I stepped in more actively. "Giselle," I said, "Dawn would like things her way. You would like things your way. You seem to feel that a person should only get her way if she has a good reason. Is that accurate?"

Giselle instinctively resisted this observation, saying she wanted Dawn to be happy. "I believe you really mean that," I said gently, "but does Dawn ever get her way when you don't feel she has a good reason?"

Giselle recalled several minor instances, but couldn't name anything of importance. Suddenly, Dawn's face lit up. "It shouldn't be Giselle's decision, should it?" she asked excitedly. "That's why I feel so crazy—I'm always having to defend myself, and Giselle makes it sound normal."

"And what happens then?" I asked encouragingly.

"Sooner or later," Dawn replied, "it becomes easier, less stressful, to do what she thinks is best."

"And," I said, completing the picture, "Giselle thinks you're doing what you want, while you don't understand why you're unhappy."

Giselle and Dawn looked at each other thoughtfully. "I don't know what we should do," Giselle said quietly, "but feeling this way is no good, is it?" They had just started to change their relationship.

Finally, sharing can support relationship or personal changes already in progress, an opportunity many of us frequently overlook. Let's say a man becomes more assertive, a change his girlfriend likes. She can now share her secret: "I've wanted you to be more dominant in bed." Her sharing supports his change.

When shouldn't you share?

Just as there are constructive reasons for speaking up, there are destructive reasons as well. Honesty that is motivated by the wrong reasons is unlikely to support the health of individuals or relationships. Instead, it often mobilizes a partner's anger, desire for retaliation, and vision of sex as a weapon.

Self-disclosure for the wrong reasons is also a form of dishonesty. While the sharing transaction may *appear* to involve closeness or regret, it may really be a disguised expression of anger. Pretending to feel one way when you actually feel another way is the classic definition of manipulation. As grand opera and soap operas alike reliably demonstrate, manipulation usually creates messy situations.

I strongly advise against using secrecy, surprise, or other dirty tactics to express strong feelings such as anger—even though at times we all feel like doing so.

Fighting dirty keeps us at the level of our childish, vulnerable feelings, unable to address issues productively. In addition, our partners frequently respond with nasty tactics of their own, which further removes everyone involved from the real issues.

If, on some level, you feel vengeful, proceed cautiously. What should you do if you feel like hurting or punishing your spouse or lover? Rather than doing it, tell him or her about *wanting* to do it. Say, for example, "Marge, when you flirt like that it makes me feel hurt and angry. Sometimes I feel like flirting with one of your friends just so you'll know how it feels. Or maybe I should even tell you about some of my past exploits so you'll feel left out just the way I do now."

This is a more productive way of handling feelings, and in all but the worst relationships, it will get your partner's attention. Make sure he or she understands that the reason you're not acting out your feelings is because your concern for the relationship is bigger than your pain—not because you're not hurt.

If you're determined to hurt your mate, do it directly and explicitly. Say, for example, "You insist on telling me about your old girlfriends even though I've begged you not to. I think it's time you heard about some of my escapades." This will make it clear that punishment is on the agenda.

Here are some other nonproductive reasons for suddenly revealing more about your sexuality:

⬩ To punish, humiliate, or get revenge: Using sensitive information to punish someone generally fails to communicate why you're so upset. And it demeans you, because you're saying, in effect, "The truth about me is so ugly that I use it as a weapon against my partner."

⬩ To relieve a heavy burden of guilt: Some people do this after a buildup of guilt, springing information on a partner unexpectedly. Others do it at the beginning of the relationship, before a trusting context has been established within which a partner could process the information. It's unfair and self-defeating to simply trade your own discomfort for your partner's. Using honesty to relieve guilt can make a relationship unnecessarily complicated and conflict-ridden.

⬩ To test the relationship: Some of us repeatedly test any relationship that seems too good to be true. We may unconsciously irritate our partner periodically to see if he or she will leave when angry; we may reveal and exaggerate our flaws early in the relationship to reduce our anxiety about being abandoned. "Reject me now," as one client recently told me, "and avoid the holiday rush."

⋄ To create a smokescreen: Some men and women reveal personal things in a colorful way to pretend that they're honest—and then go on to hide other things from a partner. For example, there are people who make it a point to gain credibility, and then proceed to have an affair, confident that they'll never be suspected.

Although honesty has the potential to improve relationships and self-image dramatically, it's also important to acknowledge unfair, hostile, and immature reasons for intimate sharing.

Resources

Anyone can make the effort to be honest about their sexuality. But doing it successfully—getting the results you want from your honesty—requires resources, both personal and relational. These resources allow two partners to use the revealed information constructively.

Almost all human beings have difficulty handling sensitive issues. We experience these difficulties through feelings like jealousy, fear, anxiety, and anger. Because of the power of these feelings, good will alone is often not enough to make honesty productive. What assets, then, should you look for as you decide on what level of honesty to operate?

COMMUNICATION

The ability and willingness to communicate is certainly your greatest asset. Good communication enables couples to use their affection, intelligence, shared history, and good intentions productively. Here are some guidelines for effective communication:

- ◇ We listen without feeling attacked or criticized.
- ◇ We can disagree without needing to destroy each other.
- ◇ We can express anger fully without needing to hurt each other.
- ◇ We feel confident that neither of us will ever become violent.
- ◇ We don't threaten or call each other nasty names.
- ◇ We generally finish important discussions without interruption or one of us storming out of the room.
- ◇ We don't fear the process of working out our disagreements.
- ◇ We don't think of anger as only destructive.
- ◇ We know how to phrase our criticism and anger in productive ways.
- ◇ We express "I care for you" frequently, both verbally and non-verbally.
- ◇ We don't bring up old hurts or irrelevant events when we disagree.
- ◇ We don't believe that disagreement means failure.

Let's look at how one couple used good communication skills to handle an extremely stressful experience of personal disclosure. The following is part of a conversation between Ashley and Tim, both doctors in their early thirties. I had not seen them since the end of our successful marital counseling the previous summer.

Ashley called, saying she wanted to come in with Tim to share something sensitive with him. She thought they could handle it alone, "But I don't want to take any chances," she said. To help you see how well they communicate, I've used brackets to highlight the clear messages within the conversation. You'll see how these helped make Ashley's honesty successful.

ASHLEY: I'm nervous about telling you this [here's how I feel], but I want to tell you because it's driving me crazy and making me feel distant from you [I want to be close to you, even while I feel upset]. You know my Uncle Harvey? He molested me for a year when I was a child. I'm sure this makes you totally upset [I'm sensitive to how you feel], but I don't want you to do anything crazy. I just want you to tell me everything's okay [here's what I want], and I want us to figure out how to deal with this [I think of us as a team].

TIM: I'm, I'm just stunned. How did this happen? How could you not tell me before now? I feel really insulted [here's how I feel]. Didn't you trust me all this time? [I'd like more information.]

ASHLEY: I guess I understand how you would feel that way [you can express your feelings without me feeling attacked]. But I just couldn't tell before. Now I can. I've changed, grown up some [I can handle your feelings without having to make you wrong]. I guess I've also gotten braver. And I believe in our marriage more [I can acknowledge loving you when things are rough].

An awkward silence filled the room, as husband and wife avoided each other's eyes. They each tried to speak once or twice, but choked back the words. Finally, Tim pounded his fist on the table. A few tears trickled down his cheek.

TIM: I'm really sorry such a terrible thing happened to you [here's how I feel]. And I'm glad you feel better having told me [I want to help ease your pain, even while I'm upset myself]. But what am I supposed to do now? I'm totally humiliated. I've been relating to this damn guy for years, not knowing how he tried to ruin my wife's life. He must think I'm either a total wimp or a complete fool [I can express my anger without needing to destroy or discredit you].

ASHLEY: I don't think he does, but I can see how you might feel that way [I know that feelings can be more important than facts; I won't try to talk you out of your feelings]. Maybe when you're less upset we can talk about that more [we finish difficult discussions].

TIM: Well, I'm going to get even with that lunatic.

ASHLEY: We need to talk about this a lot more before we do anything about it. I absolutely do not want you to go off and do something in the heat of the moment [I expect your cooperation as my partner in dealing with this issue].

There was more silence, as the two of them struggled with their feelings. As Tim's face grew darker, Ashley became scared.

ASHLEY: I'd like us to hug so I know everything is okay [I want to be close even though we're in conflict].

TIM: I'm not in the mood. I think I want to be left alone [here's what I want].

ASHLEY: Will you at least tell me you love me? [I'm willing to ask for what I want even when it's risky.]

TIM: Yeah. Of course I love you. I'm just really upset. I'll probably get over it ... I don't know how, but I suppose I will [I'm willing to stay connected with you in a small way even when we're not fully connected].

ASHLEY: Can I do anything to help?

TIM: Tell me you understand why I'm so upset [here's what I need to feel closer].

Ashley agreed, and the session proceeded. When it ended, Ashley and Tim decided they wanted to work on the issue on their own for a while. We agreed to meet again in two weeks.

Although the subject was awful, I felt proud listening to the two of them handle Ashley's revelation. Their communication wasn't perfect, but it was obviously very effective. Ashley and Tim know how to handle problems as a team, rather than as opponents.

THE RELATIONSHIP

In addition to good communication, other aspects of a strong relationship contribute to successful sharing. Here are some guidelines:

- ◇ We spend time together each week talking about things other than the kids and the household.
- ◇ We are concerned about each other's happiness and pain.
- ◇ We are each satisfied with the other's commitment to the relationship.
- ◇ We respect each other's inner experience, even if we disagree with it or don't understand it.
- ◇ We care for each other.
- ◇ We like each other.
- ◇ We each expect that our partner will deal with difficult issues without too much withdrawing, whining, or punishing.
- ◇ We both believe that our partnership is bigger than either person's temporary feelings.
- ◇ We are each able to put ourselves in the other's place, and to consider what a particular event means to him or her, rather than only to ourselves.
- ◇ We each believe that any pain the other causes is unintentional—at worst, thoughtless—rather than deliberate.

Do some or most of these qualities describe your relationship? You don't need every one of them to make sharing successful, but the more you have, the more likely it is that sharing will produce the healthy, positive results you want.

THE INDIVIDUAL

Perhaps the most important resource you can have for getting value from your sexual honesty is the sense that you're okay. Recall the Secrecy Imperative: "My sexuality and I are bad, so I must hide both." You can see that the sense of being okay makes secrecy seem far less urgent.

When you have high self-esteem, you are less likely to blame others for your bad feelings. Thus, you also would be less likely to use secrecy as a weapon, which is a demeaning thing to do. When you see yourself more as a partner or ally than as an adversary or victim, you'll think of sharing as a relationship experience, not something you do to someone else. At the same time, you will more easily handle disagreements, realizing that relationship or affection don't always require agreement.

Other personal resources that will help you to make honesty productive are intelligence, a sense of humor, patience, objectivity, and the ability to tolerate stress—all the wonderful attributes we wish we had. It reminds me of the man who spent his life looking for the perfect woman: "And when I finally found her," he said ruefully, "she was looking for the perfect man."

Why am I sharing?

As I consider sharing and being honest about my sexuality, do I have any of these good reasons?

◇ I want to get closer to my partner.

◇ I want to improve our sexual relationship.

◇ I want to increase my self-esteem.

◇ I want to reduce the physical and emotional stresses of secrecy.

◇ I want to change a relationship, or support a current change.

As I consider sharing, do I have any of these bad reasons?

◇ I want revenge.

◇ I want to punish or humiliate someone.

◇ I want to relieve a heavy burden of guilt.

◇ I want to invite criticism or punishment.

◇ I want to test a relationship.

◇ I want to create a smokescreen.

As I consider sharing, which of the following resources can I depend on?

◇ Good communication skills

◇ A good communication system

◇ A solid relationship

◇ A sense that I'm okay

◇ A sense of humor

◇ The ability to handle stress

◇ My own patience and objectivity

Preparation for sharing

So you've decided to be more honest about your sexuality—something you want, perhaps, or a fantasy or experience you've been keeping quiet about. Assuming it's for the good reasons we've discussed, congratulations. You probably feel both excited and nervous. Maybe you're also getting ready to be embarrassed, ashamed, or angry. All of these feelings are normal.

Let's discuss how to prepare for this. Ideally, you'll feel good about yourself before opening up, and you'll feel free to articulate your feelings and needs more clearly. You'll have the sense that your relationship is a cooperative partnership. And you'll arrange the kind of pragmatic support that you need, such as privacy, confidentiality, or a friendly back-rub halfway through. Particularly if you plan to reveal something big and impactful, it's important to prepare yourself, your partner, and your relationship. Being prepared means being aware of your resources, so you can use them most effectively. In this section, we will look at the forms these resources take.

Steps 1 through 7 that follow will help you recall useful information you already know, and bring together seemingly unrelated facts in helpful ways. These steps will help you transform your feelings and thoughts into resources. Step 8 then guides you through a mental rehearsal of the outcomes you hope to accomplish by sharing.

Together, the eight steps are meant to support a sense of **entitlement.** This is the sense that your needs are basically reasonable, and that your emotional reality deserves to be recognized. You don't have to earn this entitlement by being "right." Every human being is born with it, including you. Why? Simply because you are okay. Not perfect—just perfectly adequate.

Being aware of your entitlement is an important aspect of preparing for self-disclosure because it supports the loving, enlightened part of you. When an honest interaction gets difficult, a sense of entitlement also helps you keep from getting defensive. It helps you to feel close to your partner, rather than seeing him or her as an adversary.

As you look at each of the eight steps, notice how they relate to you.

1. CLARIFY YOUR GOALS

Let's start as we began Chapter 8—by examining and clarifying the goals of sharing. When you feel confident of your goals, you can fall back on them as a resource when you are confused, tongue-tied, or feeling guilty.

Elaine, for example, has a common enough secret: She wants to make love more often. Because her husband Ned has for years been considered the sex expert of the couple, Elaine hadn't even thought to assert her own needs. Instead, she harbored her desire in silence.

Elaine needed to focus on giving herself permission; specifically, making it okay to want what she wanted. Typically, Elaine judged her own needs according to the standards of others. She often feared that these standards showed that her desires were wrong.

During the course of therapy, Elaine decided to share the true level of her sexual interest. Her goals were to improve her sex life and to start asserting herself more as an equal partner with Ned. Elaine prepared for weeks before sharing. Nevertheless, the sharing itself was a difficult experience. As she told me afterward, "I got nervous and flustered when I told him, just as I feared. Ned wasn't openly angry, but he wasn't cooperative either. 'This is too hard,' I thought. 'Maybe I should just stop.'

"But I recalled what we'd discussed in session," she continued, a smile softening her face. "I remembered the goals I wrote down, the sense of direction I felt. I remembered how we had agreed that my goals were fine, even loving, and that I had no wish to hurt or insult Ned.

"So I took a deep breath, and plunged ahead. Ned was surprised and a little taken aback, I know. But we kept talking. We seem to be working things out." When Elaine began to falter in the thin air of relationship confrontation, clear goals were like extra oxygen that gave her a second wind.

2. ASSESS AND STRENGTHEN YOUR SUPPORT NETWORK

No healthy person is completely self-sufficient. We need others to support our risks and decisions, to celebrate our victories and milestones, and to sympathize with our frustrations and despair. As you deal with the stress of preparing to reveal yourself, and later with the consequences of doing so, you will appreciate the caring encouragement of others.

A support network consists of one or more people whom you can trust to help you through times of self-doubt or pain. This group may include a close friend, minister, therapist, or sister, even a whole soccer team.

When you share a sexual secret, it is often with the person whose support you normally count on the most. If he or she is upset by your revelation, that support may be least available exactly when you need it the most.

So instead of depending solely on your mate's support, consider friends, family, and co-workers. If you wish, sound them out first on a smaller issue to gauge their reaction. You may be surprised to discover who is eager to support you. If appropriate, consider seeing a professional such as a clergy member or therapist.

Books can also offer support, particularly if you feel alone or a little crazy. Some helpful titles include *Necessary Losses, It Will Never Happen to Me, Why Men Are the Way They Are, Sex is Not a Natural Act, The Erotic Impulse,* and *When Living Hurts.* As you think about revealing yourself, what kind of emotional support would you like to put in place?

3. CLARIFY YOUR VISION OF SEXUALITY

Few of us sit down and articulate our thoughts about sexuality in a coherent way. And yet we all have sexual convictions, feelings, and intuition. With the Secrecy Imperative as our heritage, sexual negativity is virtually unavoidable. While it is sometimes blatant ("fornication is a sin"), it is often more subtle (women's magazines accepting advertisments for harmful douches but not for pleasurable vibrators).

A coherent vision of sexuality is a valuable asset when you decide to live more honestly. If you view sex as wholesome, moral, and life-affirming, your beliefs can serve as guideposts when and while you share. Just as navigating a boat is easier when sailing toward a landmark or buoy, your vision can help keep you from being blown off course by having your words or intentions turned against you.

A story of my own illustrates this. The son of a friend called one day and asked to meet with me. I had watched this young man grow up over the years, and I liked him. Now a well-known freshman athlete at a big university, he was home for winter break. And he sounded troubled.

It wasn't a therapy session, so I invited him to my house. He declined a soda when he arrived, eager to talk right away. "It's the locker room," he said simply. "It's a big club, and I don't belong." I asked him to say more. "The only thing the guys ever talk about is girls," he continued. "Fine. I love talking about girls. But everyone talks about what they do with them. And because I'm a star on the field . . ." he hesitated.

"They figure you're a star off the field, too?" I suggested. Ken was relieved. "Yeah, that's it," he said. "They want to know who I sleep with, and when, and how much, and all that. But I don't . . . I haven't . . . I never . . ."

This was obviously hard for him. "Ken, lots of kids are virgins when they enter college," I said. "Many even graduate that way. There's nothing wrong with you, if that's what you're worried about."

He relaxed a bit. "Well, that's half of it," he said. "The other half is, what do I say? Should I pretend? Should I tell people to shut up? I feel really alone with this."

Feeling alone in a roomful of peers and admirers is a sad experience. "You're a big hero at school, bright and well-liked," I said. "So obviously, you've *chosen* not to have intercourse. Aside from all the pressure, do you feel okay about your choice? Does it feel like it's what's best for you? Remember, you don't need to apologize, or talk with anyone about it against your will. If a choice works for you, there's no reason to change it."

I paused and let this sink in.

"But it sure sounds like you'd appreciate sharing your dilemma with someone," I continued gently. Ken needed to feel normal within himself, and he needed a way to cope with the external pressure. "Is there a guy on the team you can trust?" I asked. "Maybe he could help you change the subject when it comes up, or deflect some of the attention. At the very least, maybe you could feel like yourself with him."

The idea delighted Ken as he started to focus on the positive aspect of his decision instead of the implied criticism in his teammates' jokes. When he used his own view of sexuality as a compass, Ken felt better about himself, and he saw how sharing his story with someone made sense. With the energy of youth, he began to plan his personal strategy immediately.

When I next saw him, during spring break, he seemed happier and more at peace with himself. He had talked to a few teammates, and found out they were uncomfortable, too. He felt less isolated, and he trusted his own judgment more and more. "Once you realize your decision is right for you," he told me, "handling other people is easier, isn't it?"

In fact, some of Ken's maturity seems to be rubbing off on the rest of the team. He says they don't pressure each other about sex nearly as much as they used to.

4. CLARIFY YOUR VISION OF THE RELATIONSHIP

Take a moment and remind yourself of the kind of relationship you desire. Luxuriate in the daydream as you create a mental image of what you'd have if your relationship were exactly as you'd like it to be—and how it would feel.

Now imagine that you're more honest in that ideal relationship than you are in the present. Perhaps your mate is frightened or angered by your honesty; perhaps he or she claims that your behavior threatens the relationship. Imagine handling this a new way, instead of getting drawn into defending yourself, which often leads to unpleasant or destructive fighting.

Instead, **you** set the terms for any conflict that arises from your sharing. Use your relationship vision to navigate the sharing experience. Invite your partner to talk about his or her perfect vision as well. As you consider the relationship you want to create, think about these issues:

- ◇ What kind of relationship rights and power do you want each of you to have?
- ◇ What kinds of roles do you want each of you to play?
- ◇ How do you want to divide relationship responsibilities?
- ◇ How much and what kind of communication do you want?
- ◇ How much routine sharing and contact do you want?

Let's look at how a relationship vision would be used during the transition to greater honesty.

Carlos was a successful carpenter who had never been married. He was sexually active and usually had several girlfriends. He "just knew I wasn't the father type. Being an uncle is perfect for me." On his thirtieth birthday he decided to get a vasectomy at the local Planned Parenthood clinic.

Four months later, Carlos's family gathered at his parents' home for Thanksgiving. The next morning, he asked his mother and father if they could sit and talk with him.

"I know you're very eager for me to raise a family," he said, "so I thought I should tell you. I've decided I'm not going to have children. I've been to a doctor and had a vasectomy. I know it's not what you wanted and you must be disappointed, but I hope you'll accept it."

After a stunned silence, Carlos's parents said everything he was afraid they would. "You're so selfish," cried his mother. "How could you run off and do such an impulsive thing?" "You'll regret being so arrogant!" his enraged father shouted. "You'll wish you hadn't thought you could predict the future. Besides, how dare you do this without talking to us first?"

Like virtually all men who have vasectomies, he was thrilled with his. Carlos hadn't had a single regret—until now, when he felt terrible. Now Carlos wanted to defend his decision, apologize for their disappointment, plead for understanding. He felt guilty, hurt, and confused.

But, as Carlos tells the story, "Then I thought, wait a minute, this makes no sense. How could this have gone from right to wrong overnight?" Carlos took a deep breath and looked directly at his parents. "Listen," he interrupted. "Listen to this so-called conversation. You say you're angry that I didn't talk to you, but here I am, talking, and you're going crazy.

"All you've done so far is tell me how stupid my decision is," he said. "You haven't asked me why I did it, what it was like, how I feel about the results, nothing." His voice shook with emotion. "*You're* hurt and angry? Well, *I'm* hurt and angry."

The room was suddenly quiet. "You two are very special to me," Carlos finally said. "I want to have a special relationship with you. But..." Carlos paused, as unhappy with the truth as he knew his parents were. "We still have a long way to go."

I think Carlos handled this situation pretty well. His mom and dad were ready to have a big fight about how wrong he was. Carlos, however, refused to get into a "bad child–angry parent" argument. Instead he stuck to his vision of the relationship he wanted with them, communicating as directly—and lovingly—as he could.

His folks will never be thrilled with his decision, but they are making progress toward resuming the satisfying relationship with their son that they used to enjoy so much. They notice and appreciate the way he loves his nieces, for example. And they're delighted with his latest gift—enlargements of some of the photos he took of the girls during the family's Christmas gathering.

5. EVALUATE AND ACCEPT YOUR FEELINGS

Knowledge, we know, is power. We generally don't apply this idea to our feelings, but when disclosing information about yourself, the more you understand your feelings, the more you can steer the interaction in the direction you want it to go.

In our noisy, fast-paced world, it may be hard to know how you really feel. Your body will tell you, if you listen: The insomnia, tight throat, pounding head, damp hands, knotted stomach, and lost (or insatiable) appetite are clear signals, **if you look and listen.** Other ways to discover your feelings include keeping a journal, going for a quiet walk every week, and watching the way others react to you.

Everyone preparing to share a secret will experience certain feelings, usually uncomfortable ones. Rather than ignoring or denying them, you're better off focusing on them. You then have a good chance of accepting and dealing with them directly. Here are some feelings you might have:

 ◇ *Fear:* I'll be judged; I'll be rejected; I'll damage my relationship.
 ◇ *Guilt:* I've done bad things; I'm bad; I've misled my partner.
 ◇ *Anger:* I can't believe I've had to hide things for so long; how dare you judge me.
 ◇ *Self-criticism:* I can't believe I was willing to lie; I'm disappointed to realize I'm so insecure; I've lied to myself.

You may also have a sense of power or pride about taking a risk, asserting your needs, stopping the lies, and restoring your integrity. The combination of guilt and pride can be confusing, but it's a normal response to emotional growth.

What does it mean to deal with your feelings? Partly, it means **stopping for a moment and experiencing your insides.** If there's hurt in there, you need to **feel** hurt. When you really feel hurt (or anxious, angry, or sad), it can be quite painful (even self-destructive) to continue with business as usual.

We all need to express how we feel. And the way the human brain is built, if we don't do it directly—by words, tears, or physical action—inevitably, we'll do it indirectly—through accidents, alcohol abuse, lowered sex drive, senseless fighting, or covertly sabotaging a partner.

The first step toward expressing your feelings is **accepting** them. Do not confuse this with liking or even approving of your feelings. You are simply embracing your inner reality, accepting what *is*. An inner voice might describe it in one of these ways:

⬦ "It's okay to feel like this."
⬦ "I know this feeling is temporary."
⬦ "I am bigger than this particular feeling."
⬦ "I have felt this way before, and gone on."
⬦ "Other reasonable people feel this way."
⬦ "This feeling is part of who I am."
⬦ "This feeling doesn't negate any other parts of me."

Accepting your feelings is accepting yourself. It helps you stay true to your goals. It helps you get through your pain, and it keeps you from assuming that just because you're uncomfortable, you're doing something wrong. When you're growing and changing, in fact, the opposite is more often true.

6. BE SENSITIVE TO YOURSELF

When you prepare to become more honest, consider your own needs and moods as well as your partner's. Respect yourself. We've talked about relaxing, feeling supported, and being clear about your goals. Here are some ways other people make their sharing experience more satisfying:

⋄ "My husband often accuses me of being undersexed, so I took a sensuous hot bath right before sharing to feel sexier."

⋄ "I was so nervous that I wasn't even sure I would go through with it, so I planned our conversation for right after my workout, when I usually feel strong."

⋄ "I was concerned about becoming bitchy about the whole thing. So to help me keep a positive attitude, I decided to talk on our anniversary, when I knew I'd be feeling close to him."

What can you do to personalize your own sharing?

7. TRANSFORM THE FEAR OF REJECTION

Certain human fears are universal: these include fear of the dark, of growing old, of the unknown, and of death. And there is fear of rejection. At no time is this fear greater than when you think about sharing a secret. We've already looked at the source and expression of this fear. Let's now look at it as a source of energy to be transformed and used.

To do so we have to look beneath the surface, at what lies closest to the fear of rejection: First, our desire for closeness and connection. Second, our idealization of another person (if not for these, rejection would not pose such a profound threat). Third, our self-criticism—our sense that we deserve rejection, on some level, fueling our fear that it will happen.

Whether they make sense or not, these primitive emotions drive our fear—unless we deal with them consciously. So you must interrupt your fear, getting to the feelings beneath it. Then you can remind yourself of your good intentions (to feel close); of your highest aspirations (your idealizations of your partner); and of your reflexive negativity (your self-criticism). If you do this, you will short-circuit your own fears. You'll soon start noticing how much less you say, "I can't help it; I just feel afraid."

One way to be aware of your emotions is by examining your assumptions about the sharing interaction. What do you suppose will happen? How do you imagine your partner will feel? How will he or she respond to you? How will you handle that response? What will be the long-term results? Does this feel like a painful situation you've been in before? Do you think things will unfold this time as they did then? And are you scaring yourself as you think this over? Rehearsing failure?

If we were like *Star Trek's* Mr. Spock, we would anticipate the future using accurate data and perfect logic. Instead, our judgment is normally colored by simple human fears and desires. We can prepare for being more open by examining our assumptions about ourselves and our partners.

Then take a Mr. Spock-like attitude: How likely is it, **really,** that my boyfriend will yell at me, that I will fall apart when he yells, that he will leave me when I do? Or, how likely is it, **really,** that my daughter will tell me she's disgusted, refusing to meet my new lover? Lay out your own worst-case scenarios and evaluate their likelihood. You'll almost certainly find that the facts suggest a milder outcome than you fear.

The other way to handle your fears is to discuss them. Tell your lover that you fear rejection, explaining what lies behind that for you. Talking about your desire for closeness and your fear of losing it can be one of the most intimate moments in any relationship. Emotional energy is powerful; use it consciously. Instead of letting it isolate you through fear, use it to create connection.

Reinforcing your relationship by talking about your fears sets the stage for disclosing about yourself more effectively.

8. REHEARSE AND VISUALIZE SHARING

Bernie Zilbergeld wrote in *Mind Power* that positive mental rehearsal can improve performance in virtually all of life's tasks. World-class athletes have been "visualizing" for years now, with startling results. You can, too.

The first stage is to **practice** being relaxed. To start with, just breathe a little more slowly and deeply. Drop your shoulders and let your jaw go slack. Feel the warm sense of well-being this produces in your body. You can create this relaxed sensation at will under any circumstance, simply by choosing to do so. Resolve now that you'll remember to do it as you begin to share.

Now close your eyes. Imagine telling your partner about yourself, and notice how you're maintaining your composure under stress. You're breathing, even smiling occasionally, feeling confident and focused on your goals. Visit this fantasy for thirty seconds each day before you talk about something scary. It will help you create the reality you desire.

Now that you've rehearsed mentally, do it physically. You may feel silly at first, but this step really does help. Imagine you're with the person you'll be speaking to. Begin your conversation out loud. Say a few words you're likely to start with, like "Wendy, this is awkward for me, but I really want to talk about what's on my mind." Or "Brad, I want to tell you something that will probably surprise you. I'd like you to just listen until I'm finished."

Note your tone of voice, manner of standing or sitting, gestures and other forms of presentation. Start speaking out loud again, adjusting your style to better reflect your intentions. Want to be more assertive? Rehearse speaking that way, as if you already are more assertive. Practice and repetition will help make it so.

Finally, visualize—mentally rehearse—getting the results you want. This may include being understood in a new way, negotiating specific relationship changes, having a deeper sense of closeness with the other person, or feeling proud of yourself. If the image doesn't come easily, take a deep breath and stay with it. Above all, if you can only visualize problems and drama resulting from your honesty, take some time to imagine a different, positive ending. Don't be one of those people who can't take *yes* for an answer.

Preparing your partner and your relationship

The goal of this section is to assist you in the following:

◇ Recall and reaffirm the special bond, history, and resources you and your partner have together (regardless of the kind of relationship it is).

◇ Think of yourselves as a problem-solving **team,** rather than as individuals with competing interests.
Keeping these two points in mind increases your chances of creating positive results. Start by asking yourself what typically nurtures your relationship. It may be a walk in the park, a half-hour with a photo album, reading together in bed, or something else. It will be instructive to think about this; so will discussing it with your partner. You'll be looking at the nuts and bolts of intimacy.

Then actually do one or more of these activities prior to disclosing something difficult. It will help create a warm, cooperative atmosphere. Next, look at and clean up the communication in your relationship.

Discuss the nonverbal ways you two "talk" to each other, along with what various behaviors usually mean. Sometimes we use behavior to convey things that we're not willing to say directly, which can make a partner resentful. Do you:

◇ Busy yourself with chores when a partner wants your company?
◇ Read the paper while someone speaks to you?
◇ Distract the speaker by stroking him or her seductively?
◇ Nervously tap, tear, or play with nearby objects while being spoken to?
◇ Roll your eyes or make faces? (When done repeatedly, partners usually respond by calling it "that face.")
◇ Correct the speaker's grammar when he or she is explaining something important?

When people experience such behaviors, they typically feel patronized, unsupported, dismissed, distanced, or manipulated. If so, complaining "that's not what I meant" won't help much. If your partner feels demeaned, that *is* the communication, especially if it happens again and again.

Partners rarely discuss their nonverbal communication. Instead, most of us assume that we know what these gestures mean. To help make your sharing more effective, explore the nonverbal communication in your relationship. Start by talking about an old misunderstanding you've resolved, or a question you have now.

Similarly, attend to the verbal component of your relationship. While we like to think that we understand each other's words, this isn't always true.

Do you generally feel understood by your partner? If not, discuss this with him or her. Your goal is not to decide who to blame, but rather to explore how you feel, what the results are, and how to improve this outcome. Only then can you begin to change the communication system.

For example, do one or both of you interrupt frequently? Do you feel you don't always get your turn to speak? Do you wish your partner gave you more feedback? Perhaps you desire a different kind of response. Instead of empathizing with others, for example, many people try to fix their feelings. They may try to convince someone—perhaps you—that there's no reason to be upset; warn that it doesn't look good to cry in public; or try to solve a problem before you're ready, and so on.

Do either of you use particular words or expressions that always irritate or hurt the other? Some parents nag their children about not living up to their "potential." Some wives criticize their husbands' lack of "manliness," while many men complain that their wives are "too emotional."

When particular words or phrases acquire a negative history between two people, they disrupt and eventually prevent productive communication. Take a moment to list a few such words in one or more of your relationships. Share the list with your partners, who may want to add a few. Agree to use different, neutral terms whenever possible. Here are some examples of "loaded" words and expressions:

- ♦ Tolerant
- ♦ Selfish
- ♦ Mama's boy
- ♦ Drama queen
- ♦ A real man
- ♦ A real wife
- ♦ A little more patience
- ♦ Try harder
- ♦ A real killjoy
- ♦ A stick-in-the-mud

⟡ Too kinky
⟡ Be more cooperative

Different terms, of course, are sensitive for different people.

The next step in preparing your partner for new levels of honesty and intimacy is to assure him or her of your commitment. Tell your partner explicitly that your intention is to communicate, not to criticize or punish. Let him or her know that you care about the feelings your honesty may kindle in him or her. For example, "Jim, this will be hard for me, so I imagine it will be hard for you. I promise to listen to everything you have to say about it—I really want to know what you think." This will help your partner avoid feeling like your adversary.

Most people have anxiety about this process, and sharing that with your partner is almost always appropriate. It activates your partner's natural concern for you, and also helps him or her know that you're not just coldly plowing ahead without concern. Keep in mind, as we have noted before, that **talking about your anxiety tends to reduce it.**

Talking about yourself in new ways will probably create some stress for you. What are the results of the ways you handle stress? Do they make the problem worse? Do they reinforce a feeling of powerlessness? Do they make the return of stress inevitable?

How do you and your partner handle stress? Here are some common scenarios:

⟡ "I just try to ignore it, pretend it's not there."
⟡ "We make love."
⟡ "We bring up old arguments."
⟡ "I eat, usually stuff I shouldn't."
⟡ "I spend money."
⟡ "We focus on the kids, either positively or negatively."

⬦ "We watch TV as a way of taking time out from each other."
⬦ "One or both of us has a drink."
⬦ "We invite other people over and relate to them."
⬦ "We do a few chores or catch up on some office work."

What better ways can you think of to handle relationship stress? You may find it helpful to ask your partner (spouse, child, colleague) to brainstorm with you. One way to do this is to recall, together, times when you handled difficult situations as a team. You might have talked long into the night several times in a week, or spent a day at the beach thinking about things, or even bought a book or consulted an expert.

Most relationships have at least a few successful experiences, even if they happened long ago. You each felt heard then, didn't you? And you felt like partners, right? Remembering this feeling is a good step toward recreating it.

When you've come this far, you have prepared your partner and your relationship. Love or trust, in some form, should be in the air. Your team's resources should be familiar and more easily accessible. Sharing is becoming a greater possibility every moment. To reward yourself for working so hard, go for a walk someplace pretty. There's more work to do when you return.

Think about it:

As I prepare to share, which of the following have I done:

> Have I clarified my goals?
>
> Have I assessed and strengthened (if necessary) my support network?
>
> Have I clarified my vision of sexuality?
>
> Have I clarified my vision of the relationship?
>
> Have I evaluated and accepted my feelings, needs, and moods?
>
> Have I examined and worked on my fear of rejection?
>
> Have I rehearsed and visualized sharing?
>
> Have I acknowledged my fears?
>
> Have I thought about whose problem the anticipated consequences will be?
>
> Have I thought about the consequences of **not** sharing?

As I prepare to share, I think about the following:

> What activities usually nurture our relationship?
>
> How can I clean up the communication in our relationship (both verbal and nonverbal)?
>
> How can I reassure my partner of my commitment to our relationship?
>
> How should I prepare to handle the stress of sharing?

As I prepare to share, I think about choosing the following circumstances:

> Neither of us has been drinking.
> We are not in the middle of a serious argument.
> We have enough time to explore and handle the resulting situa-
> tion.
> We have enough privacy.
> We have whatever level of confidentiality we need.

Chapter 9

(Finally) Getting Beyond Orgasm

☉☉

Sex is one of nine good reasons for reincarnation. The other eight reasons aren't important.

—HENRY MILLER

We've looked at your desire to be normal, the typical reaction of withholding your true self and the effects of this on your relationships and sexual experiences. We've looked at how to take risks and honestly share parts of your erotic self, a tantalizing hint of what's possible once you accept yourself.

So let's get back to sex. If you bring your whole self to bed, if you're not simply trying to get through sex without making a mess or looking foolish, what's actually possible? What's beyond orgasm?

What is sex for—now?

Let's start with some new goals. If sex is not about performance or proving that you're a real man or a real woman, what does sex have to offer?

For openers, of course, there's pleasure. To maximize sexual pleasure, we need to be emotionally present, rather than distracted by either anxiety or the need to accomplish things. You may also desire and enjoy closeness as a sexual goal. You can pursue it from a sense of desperation or from the desire to limit erotic intensity. Or you can welcome it from a more relaxed place of openness and willingness to know and be known by another person. In fact, feeling known is itself a wonderful goal for sex. You can have this experience only if you really show yourself to your partner, rather than pretending to be someone else—say, someone more "ladylike," or less "kinky," or more "manly," or less "straight."

If you are more relaxed, honest about who you are, and confident that whatever happens sexually will be okay, you can then use sexuality to approach additional ends. Sex can become a vehicle for self-expression—a way to use your body to express who you are, how you feel, and your relationship to others. Similarly, sexuality can be a platform from which you explore the world. This can include fantasies, the sound of your own voice saying nasty things, the use of everyday places and situations as sexy ones (elevators, shoe stores, dining out, window shopping), and new erotic positions. All this is possible when you have no preconceived limits about what is or isn't sexual.

It shouldn't need saying, but let's say it out loud anyway: None of these goals for sex are any "better" than any others; none of them are necessary for enjoyable sex; we shouldn't expect to have all of these gratifications every time we have sex; and working hard and being anxious to accomplish any of these things defeats the spirit of the kind of sex they're part of.

Creating a new kind of erotic experience that will nourish us and provide entry to new worlds obviously requires leaving behind some mental baggage. In this case, what dearly held beliefs about sex—what myths that almost everyone believes—must we let go of? We began our erotic journey by identifying and discussing several popular myths. Let's conclude our journey in the same way—by identifying some dearly held, culturally sanctioned ideas about sex that need to be left behind for anyone taking the path beyond orgasm.

MYTH: ORGASM IS THE GOAL OF SEX

When you consider the various activities that typically take place during sexual encounters, such as undressing, kissing, laughing, looking, smelling, whispering, tasting, and touching, it's amazing that we focus so much on the eight-second activity that comes at the end of all this (if, in fact, it does happen). Although no one can deny the exquisite pleasure of a guilt-free orgasm, it's curious that so many of us actually behave as if that's the reason we create complicated, time-consuming sexual encounters in the first place.

I don't believe that we are obsessed with orgasm only because of the physical pleasure it affords. Rather, I think that for many people orgasm is a symbolic moment—of sexual adequacy, success, and meaning. If this is the case, seeing orgasm as the goal of sex makes sense. If, on the other hand, you can derive a variety of physical and psychological payoffs from the entire erotic experience, orgasm is just one more feature of sex—and not always the most exciting or enjoyable.

While we're on the subject, let's debunk some other myths about orgasm.

MYTH: SIMULTANEOUS ORGASM IS THE BEST KIND

Partners coming at the same time is, first of all, rather unusual. Synchronizing the involuntary reflexes of two bodies is quite a trick, and frequently way more trouble than it's worth. It does not represent some apex of sexual skill or collaboration with a lover. And frankly, it can be quite distracting to have your partner involved in the throes of passion at the same moment that you're abandoning yourself to your own orgasm. In fact, how can we expect anyone to continue giving us the stimulation we love during our orgasm if they're wildly involved in their own? Similarly, it can be difficult to keep stimulating your partner in exactly the way he or she wants when you're surrendering to your own impending climax.

Unmask the Myth:

Thirty years ago, well-known psychiatrist Dr. Thomas Szasz challenged the way his own profession had been promoting an unrealistic model of sexual adequacy: "The modern erotic ideal: man and woman in loving sexual embrace, experiencing simultaneous orgasm through genital intercourse. This is a psychiatric-sexual myth useful for fostering feelings of sexual inadequacy and personal inferiority. It is also a rich source of psychiatric 'patients.' "

Instead of working so hard (and being distracted) to achieve some fabled height of intimacy, slow down, relax, and match your partner's breathing. This will coordinate your body with your lover's and provide an actual experience of stress-free closeness in a natural, unforced way. You might even have more exciting orgasms in the process.

Myth: Multiple orgasms should be every woman's goal

Let's also say out loud that multiple orgasms are not the ultimate form of sexual peak (multiple orgasms involve coming more than once without completely cooling off in between). Many women's bodies just don't do this. Some women find multiple orgasms distracting—getting excited again when they want to settle down and cuddle—and some couples find them disruptive, making it hard to sustain a mutual rhythm. Mostly, women (and a few men) who strive for multiple orgasms, or their partners who struggle to create them, limit their ability to be present and really feel the physical and emotional experience of lovemaking.

Working hard to achieve *any* kind of sex is a choice that invites frustration and limited responsiveness.

UNMASK THE MYTH:

Breathing is a key to multiple orgasms—tolerating the arousal as it builds. On the other hand, this should be a means, not an end in itself. When you see it this way, you can ask (and answer truthfully) "Is what I'm doing to create this worth the effort?"

MYTH: MEN DON'T ENJOY SEX WITHOUT ORGASM

Can a man enjoy sex if he doesn't come? Few twenty-year-olds have mastered this trick, but many forty- and fifty-year-olds find themselves developing the attitude necessary to do so. It's a good thing, because one of the ways men's bodies often change as they age is that orgasms are no longer inevitable even with perfect stimulation.

UNMASK THE MYTH:

Some people are committed to the idea that if they don't come, they can't possibly enjoy sex. Contrary to the propaganda that many high school and college men spread, a highly aroused male body can do fine without an orgasm. So go and enjoy it, and take your partner with you— a guided tour of your balls, mutual massage, running your hair all over your partner. Most of all, kiss while you're being sexual together. A lot. Enjoyable kissing puts people in altered states during which they are less judgmental, more open, and more sexually creative.

MYTH: THERE'S A HIERARCHY OF SEXUAL ACTIVITIES

As we've discussed, many of us think of intercourse as "real sex" and of everything else as "foreplay." We may also consider genital activities, such as oral sex and hand jobs, to be closer to "real sex" than nongenital activities like kissing, caressing, cuddling, licking, and biting.

This kind of approach encourages score-keeping and performance evaluations that are separate from the sexual experiences themselves. And it makes you push beyond what you may actually enjoy to get to the "real thing" whether it's appropriate or not, or even whether it gives you more pleasure or not. It also makes it more likely you'll find yourselves in a sexual rut sooner or later.

What a shame. You can't go beyond orgasm if you can't enjoy what you're doing without an eye focused somewhere else.

UNMASK THE MYTH:

Pay attention to what you're doing while you're doing it. Ask your lover how it feels. Then tell your lover how it makes you feel. This will help you both slow down and stay in the moment.

MYTH: IT'S BEST IF YOU CAN HAVE GOOD SEX WITHOUT "COMMUNICATION"

You can enjoy sex without communicating with your lover—as long as you don't expect too much out of the experience. However, most of the emotional gratifications we want from sex are possible only with clear communication. Helping your partner feel comfortable, close, and excited almost invariably requires this too, and so does experimentation.

Why do so many of us seem to resent this fact? I think it's because communicating requires you to acknowledge that you're really there, being sexual, with the person you're actually with. That's a lot of things to be honest with yourself about, and not everyone is up to it. But this is the kind of honesty that's required if you're going to go beyond orgasm.

UNMASK THE MYTH:

No one claims that communication undermines the experience of non-sexual activities. Nor does anyone think that a nonsexual relationship is superior if it is accomplished without communication. In fact, the opposite is frequently true. Think, for example, of cooking, shopping, or tennis.

Talking, touching, holding, and kissing with your eyes open will help you find and keep your bearings so you can lose yourself in passion.

MYTH: SEXUAL ABILITY DECLINES WITH AGE, ESPECIALLY FOR MEN

This is a combination of urban legend, misquoted science, and narrow thinking. It's only true if you define "sexual ability" as the strengths that twenty-year-olds bring to sex, which are physical energy, great reflexes, and the lack of physical limitations. This typically translates into quick and hard erections, thick and plentiful lubrication, plenty of tireless thrusting, and the absence of medication side effects.

On the other hand, if we define "sexual ability" as enthusiasm, communication, sense of humor, self-knowledge, experience with various partners, and life skills that give us perspective, not only don't our sexual abilities decline with age, they actually increase. No wonder people in mid-life can go beyond orgasm far, far more easily than young adults.

UNMASK THE MYTH:

Use it or lose it? Some of the changes that come with age can be inconvenient—a longer refractory period between ejaculation and erection, for for example. However, many others can actually enhance your experience—lasting longer before ejaculation, understanding that thrusting isn't everything, etc. Once you get past the mental baggage that physical change inevitably means you're losing your sexuality, you can use your sense of humor, experience, and creativity to take advantage of them.

MYTH: SEX SHOULD PROCEED IN AN ORDERLY, LINEAR FASHION

Most of us like to know where we are and where we're going. That's why we prefer sex to go in a straight line: a predictable buildup of excitement that continues without "interruption," a sequence of activities aimed toward the strictly genital, and an increasing loss of self-consciousness. The media tell us that not only is this desirable, but that it's possible, and that other kinds of sex are inferior.

In real life, however, arousal, response, and focus ebb and flow during sexual encounters. Contraception and lubricants, bathroom breaks, conversation or laughter, and logistical issues like ringing telephones, restless children, and leg cramps are part of sex—not interruptions, but part of it. The more we expect such experiences during sex, and accept the need to create a sexual rhythm that accommodates them, the easier it is to enjoy sex and to go beyond orgasm.

It turns out that gourmet sex is similar to gourmet cooking: You don't have to mess up the place, but it's nice to know you can.

UNMASK THE MYTH:

One option: Try incorporating any potential distractions into your lovemaking. Phone ringing? Caressing your partner's butt while she talks to the babysitter on the phone can be exciting for both of you. Leg cramp need a sudden massage? Don't stop when the cramp does. Penis and balls too stale to lick? A warm, wet wash cloth can be a wonderful prelude to some head.

MYTH: SEX EITHER EXPRESSES LOVE OR IS MEANINGLESS

As we've seen, many of us would like sex to be simpler than it really is. Put another way, we would like sexuality to validate our existing feelings and assumptions about people, society, religion, and gender.

The ideals of romantic love and of sexuality as an expression of that romantic love are only a few centuries old. Many people, however, feel that there is some fundamental truth or natural law that makes this the only valid kind of sexual expression.

Whether instructed through the religious, legal, medical, or psychiatric professions, many of us assume that sex which does not validate a heterosexual, monogamous union is meaningless. Not that there's anything wrong with meaningless sex—as meaningless experiences go, sex is pretty fine.

But there are many, many forms of sexual relating that are neither a validation of a loving union **nor** meaningless. Even sex with someone you barely know can be intense, intimate, and revelatory. We all know about casual sex that starts in bars and at resorts. Perhaps you know that millions of Americans are part of a loose community (swingers) in which groups of consenting adults gather regularly to have sex with each other. They find this growth-producing, life-enhancing, and even supportive of their intimate relationships, in addition to intensely pleasurable.

Finally, there are an increasing number of people involved in commercial sex or Internet sex who have a wide range of subjective experiences that are demeaned by the simplistic, false dichotomy of "loving sex vs. meaningless sex."

UNMASK THE MYTH:

There are many different experiments you might want to try in this arena, depending on what you need and how fast you can grow.

For example, you can ask yourself what you're trying to accomplish by persuading yourself that a given sexual encounter has "meaning." Or you can discard everything you think about the connection between love, sex, and intimacy, and craft a model from scratch. It may end up looking just like your current model, but it'll be easier to own when you recreate it consciously.

Outercourse

Another way to describe the kind of sex that takes you beyond orgasm is outercourse. This is in contrast to intercourse, the benchmark for describing conventional sex (which divides all erotic activity into either "real sex" or "foreplay"). During intercourse-oriented sexual activity, most people have a fairly good idea of where they are: foreplay, intercourse, or "afterwards."

In outercourse, however, there's less of a set routine or pattern, and no narrative arc, and so participants don't typically know exactly where they are. If you are one of those people who need to keep their bearings during sex, this may make you anxious, or you could consider it an advantage. Are you willing to consciously lose track, during sex, of exactly what's happening, of whose body parts are whose, and of other psychological anchors such as clarity about time and space? If so, outercourse offers virtually limitless options.

But if there is little or no narrative arc to sexual experiences oriented to outercourse, how do you know what to do? The challenging answer is that there is nothing to do, and so you just do whatever feels good. Yes, within the values context of honesty, consent, and responsibility, you really can have sex where anything goes, in which personal preferences of the moment rule. That's the path to the place beyond orgasm.

Sexual "problems"

What then, of the common problems that people experience during sex? How do you get beyond orgasm when you can't even get it up, or get wet?

For better or worse, almost everyone experiences unwanted surprises, disappointments, and limitations at some point or other during even the best sex. *Really satisfying sex does not depend on the absence of these difficulties, but rather on the way that people handle them when they show up.* Those who know how to make sex their own, rather than slavishly feeling compelled to "do sex right," simply make room for whatever comes along.

So—erection or lubrication difficulty? Do something sexual that doesn't require erections or lubrication, or use artificial substitutes for each.

A lover who refuses to do your favorite activity, or whose body simply can't? Find other ways to thrill yourself and your partner. Grieve the loss of your favorite activity until you've accepted it and moved on emotionally.

Chronic or sporadic pain that eliminates the pleasure from certain sexual activities or positions? Same thing.

Side effects of prescription medications such as antidepressants, antihypertensives, hormone replacement therapy, diuretics? Same thing.

That is, just ignore these various circumstances and do the things that typically constitute healthy sexuality:

- ◇ Communicate.
- ◇ Know your preferences.
- ◇ Be in the moment.
- ◇ Forego sexual goals and performance.

The ups and downs of life require a work-around in sex, regardless of what form they take. Simple? Yes. Simplistic? No.

Remember, once you anticipate and take responsibility for the consequences of your erotic choices, nothing can go wrong during sex.

Being yourself—beyond judgments

The erotic state we're exploring here is one in which you have access to your self as you really are. Once you admit your eroticism to yourself—fantasies, preferences, experiences, choices—you can relax. You can no longer fool yourself, and if you don't mistreat others, you don't need to judge yourself. In fact, you don't need to worry about sexual partners judging you, because you already accept yourself.

From the safety of self-acceptance, why would you judge a partner's sexuality? Your lover's body, preferences, fantasies, and limitations aren't about you, don't threaten to make you feel bad, so it's easier to accept them. And so, ultimately, you can hear what he or she has to say much more easily. Whether it's "Yes, please do this" or "No, I don't want to," when you feel erotically secure you can simply say, "Tell me more."

Sex as spiritual practice

Once you stop trying to have "successful" sex, and choose sex without the distractions of performance anxiety, comparisons with the past, or the need to control how you're seen by your partner, sex can be a sacred practice. You can focus on your breathing, the sensuality of your experience, and the purity of your eroticism. With everything else stripped away, when nothing else has meaning or substance, sexuality is revealed in its pure essence, which your body can inhabit. Your body becomes a vessel that can be filled with erotic spirit. This is the kind of experience you can have that, indeed, lies beyond anything that orgasm offers.

There's a spiritual quality to such an attitude, a peacefulness and sense of connectedness to the world and to your lover. In fact, erotic self-acceptance and an openness to the existence of a wider erotic world (regardless of how much of it you actually want to taste) is the gateway to other spiritual aspects of sexuality.

Sex offers an opportunity to experience the perfection of your body. No one feels fat during such an erotic journey. No one judges sagging breasts. "Sagging" itself becomes an irrelevant judgment; your partner's breasts are simply there, ready to be enjoyed—if you choose. This can last at least as long as the sexual encounter itself—way, way more than the eight pulsing seconds of orgasm. In the context of living in a youth-obsessed culture, periodic experiences of our body's perfection have great healing power that lasts well beyond sex itself.

Beyond orgasm

In comparison with erotic purity and our body's perfection, time itself seems like a pretty trivial matter. In more conventional sex, time is often suspended for the seven or eight seconds that orgasm typically lasts. Beyond orgasm are erotic experiences in which time may seem suspended much, much longer.

Self-acceptance and the honesty it makes feasible take us to the threshold of a new kind of sex. Timelessness, spirituality, experimentation without criticism, and a dramatic expansion of what seems erotic and possible: That's what lies beyond orgasm.

Mars? Venus? or Earth?

⊚⊚

Perhaps you've noticed that there's no advice in this book directed specifically to men or to women. Well, it's no oversight. After twenty-two years in clinical practice, and a half-million visitors to my website, it seems clear: male sexuality and female sexuality are far more similar than different. To put it another way, the similarities between male and female sexuality are far more important than the differences.

I know that for some people, this is radical thinking. After all, one of the most popular books of our time is *Men Are from Mars, Women Are from Venus*. With all due respect to those who love this book's basic idea, it's important to recognize its limitations.

For starters, the Mars/Venus model stereotypes men and women. During your life, you'll definitely meet people who fit these stereotypes and you'll definitely meet others who don't. For example, in half the couples I see with desire problems, it's the woman who wants sex more than the man. In half the couples I see in which someone wants more communication, it's the man.

You know, no one is in love with the "average man" or the "average woman" (who don't, after all, exist), and no one has sex with this myth-ical creature. Thus, trying to understand "men" or "women" isn't very valuable. You'd be a lot better off trying to understand Joe or Mary.

And there's another way in which the mythical average man and average woman aren't helpful. The range of what men like, think, feel, and want is extraordinarily broad, covering practically everything. The same is true of women. They are a very, very mixed group, whose tastes vary tremendously.

Imagine two men, one of whom wants sex every day and the other of whom wants sex once a year. In such a sample, the average man would want sex every other day—which wouldn't help you understand the second one at all. Similarly, if you hear that the average woman wants oral sex twice per month, and you're with a woman who doesn't want it at all, the average is of no help whatsoever. And how do you take the "average" of three people: one of whom enjoys S/M, one who likes to make love listening to Sinatra, and one who's never had an orgasm?

Ultimately, there's more variation among all men and there's more variation among all women then there is between the so-called average man and the so-called average woman.

Instead, we should be looking at the similarities between male and female sexuality. Most people of each gender:

⋄ Want to feel good in their bodies.
⋄ Enjoy some level of touching.
⋄ Like to feel desired.
⋄ Like to feel desire.
⋄ Want sex to be easy and simple.
⋄ Enjoy sexual arousal and satisfaction.
⋄ Experience sexual side effects from common medications.
⋄ Have some confusion about their own body.
⋄ Are concerned about being sexually normal.
⋄ Feel some inhibition discussing about sexuality.
⋄ Believe that other people are more comfortable with sex, and are having it more often.

◇ Are curious about others' sexuality, but don't ask questions.
◇ Go through changes in sexual function as they age.
◇ Are concerned about losing their attractiveness over time.

When we look at similarities such as these, we realize that women and men are both from Earth—a sexually troubled planet with the potential for tremendous erotic enjoyment and closeness—beyond orgasm.

Index